Authentic Guts

Authentic Guts

THIS IS A SANKOFA ACHIEVEMENT CENTER, INC.
BOOK
PUBLISHED BY DR. APRIL A. JONES

Copyright ©

2021 by SAC Publishing
All rights reserved. Published in the United States by Dr. April A. Jones, a division of Sankofa Achievement Center Inc.
Nashville, Tennessee.

www.thesac.org
Library of Congress Cataloging-Publication Data
Names: Dr. April A. Jones, Author.
Title: Authentic Guts: Culturally Relevant Best Practices For Reaching The Youth "At Risk."
Identifiers ISBN-9781737993018 (ebook), ISBN-9781737993001 (print hardback), ISBN-9781737993032 (print paperback)

Jacket Illustration: Carl Burrell
Editor: Cynthia G. Jones
Guest Editor: Janie Taylor
Foreword: Faatymah Kitt

Manufactured in the United States of America

FOREWORD

Written by Faatymah Kitt

The struggle has been very real from the beginning. Since pre-k, no even earlier daycare, my son's and my walk through the education system has been met with challenges. My son was diagnosed with ADHD after repeated incidents at daycares. I noticed my son had extreme busy body behaviors and impulsiveness that led me to seek a medical opinion. After filling out questionnaires and being examined, it was suggested I place him on medication. I thought that was a bit extreme and I refused to medicate him. I sought alternative means via diet and vitamins to help him. He had an extraordinary challenge remaining still in class or on topic. Public schooling began to tear at his self esteem.

They began to place him in categories with labels I didn't know what to do with because at home, he's a bright intelligent boy who can't sit still, but by no means a bad, disrespectful, ignorant, or uncontrollable child. These words were becoming common in describing him from his teachers. I knew something was wrong. Luckily, I had a teacher on my side who happened to be my best friend and god mother to my son. She had always helped and guided me in my role as his advocate in countless meetings with teachers, principals, doctors, and outside behavior organizations. My struggle with ensuring my son's education and empowerment was the inspiration behind the poem written below.

I write his name on his ball
Real Big
So he won't lose it
Name written on his dreams so there's no bluesing it
I teach him the game so *Yes!* he can use it
A Mother's love is the best gift I own
Make a grizzly monster of me disturbing the powerful growth to his throne

Patience is thin
It's a *No* to standing idle
No sideline watching him losing
When *the* system is bruising
Judging fish cuz their losing on the track
Making his whole life about his inability to run
When "*it's*" the system that's dumb, numb, *n'* overcome

I know a change is going to come
Every child should get saved not just the lucky ones
Let's "*Blessed!*" them all
Let's brighten up days bring up right raise chins up to the sky
Build strong backs heads up high
Young Kings, Young Queens are who we're raising

Thankful for a higher power or we would be lost
Thankful for graceful saviors that lessen the cost
But how does it go when it all falls down, all the try fails
When the lucks run out when the loves all gone
When wounded babes get tossed and turned in a system geared toward demise
We know how this goes it's no surprise
The state of our jails-it's a pipeline
We've read all these doctored books, taught lessons full of holes
We know what comes
It's the present gory nightmare of today's risen sun
We few, we bold that make it to *Grace* are just the lucky ones
Lucky green, my black fist high
Children of the sun, we do not die in vain
We carry your names like torches as we press forward on this path for change

FAATYMAH KITT @FKITTARTIST

ACKNOWLEDGMENTS

I would like to first thank the Almighty Creator for continuing to give me good health. The health of self-love most importantly. Second, I would like to thank my mother for grounding and instilling discipline for academia in me. I wasn't allowed to bring home a grade less than a 'B or else it was going to be hell to pay. Although some of her methods of discipline were a bit drastic; borderline child abuse if you ask me, but she always said *"But look how you turned out!"* Like the old folks say, *"she kept her foot in my ass,"* lol.

Next, I would like to thank my beautiful intelligent and well-disciplined children for supporting me and following my footprints towards academic excellence. Keep striving and reaching for the stars you two. I'm super proud of you.

Thank you Mrs. Lestine Vines, Ms. Purnell, and all my other wonderful teachers from Florence B. Price Elementary School in Chicago, Illinois. I would like to thank all of my close family, friends and the parents who have supported me. They've been my number one fans and advocates from the beginning of my aspirations. Thank you Venise, you have the patience of Job, lol. Professor Mrs.Wanda Burrell thank you for your motivation. Roxanne Ross I needed the opportunity to teach and you gave it to me at Whitsett Elementary. Sarah Bradburn thank you for your inspiring notes that still hang on my walls. Pat Blankenship, Norma Yoos, Carl Burrell, and Angela Varnadoe - My board of directors of the SAC from the beginning of incorporation, thank you for believing in the vision.

Outside the communication tent where I worked and slept in Kandahar, Afghanistan 2002

Dr. April A. Jones
EXECUTIVE DIRECTOR
WWW.THESAC.ORG

TABLE OF CONTENTS

INTRODUCTION	1
PART I:	
AUTHENTIC GUTS	3
PERSONAL TO PRACTICE	9
PART II: BEST PRACTICES FOR ALL STUDENTS	
EDUCATION	22
RESEARCH ON CULTURAL RELEVANCY IN URBAN COMMUNITIES	33
PART III: PERSPECTIVE ON INCLUSION	
PHILOSOPHY OF COLLABORATIVE TEACHING IN INCLUSIVE CLASSROOMS	45
PART IV: RESEARCH-BASED STRATEGIES FOR ENGAGING EXTERNAL PARTNERS FOR STUDENT SUCCESS	
COMMUNITY PARTNERSHIPS IN RURAL COMMUNITIES	57
PART V: FUTURE DIRECTIONS	
CLOSING COMMENTS	78
REFERENCES	81
DESCRIPTION OF THE BOOK COVER DESIGN	92

HI, I'M APRIL

April A. Jones Ed. D - Tennessee State University
2021

Sankofa Achievement Center, Inc.
Executive Director
Nashville, TN 2011
www.thesac.org

About me

The following text is excerpted from "A Torchlight for America," chapter 4, pages 47-53, written by the Honorable Minister Louis Farrakhan, 1993.]

In The Name of Allah, The Beneficent, The Merciful.
Let's deal with what education is supposed to be as opposed to what it is in America. One of the things that separates man from beast is knowledge. Knowledge feeds the development of the human being so that the person can grow and evolve into Divine and become one with The Creator. It's not one's maleness or femaleness, being Black or being White, rather it is our growth and reflection of knowledge that distinguishes us from the lower forms of life.

Education is supposed to be the proper cultivation of the gifts and talents of the individual through the acquisition of knowledge. Knowledge satisfies our natural thirst for gaining that which will make us one with our Maker. So true education cultivates the person—mind, body and spirit—by bringing us closer to fulfilling our purpose for being, which is to reflect Allah (God).
The second purpose for education, after self-cultivation, is to teach us how to give proper service to self, family, community, nation and then to the world.

The problem in today's education is that the root motivation is the acquisition of wealth and material things rather than cultivation of the human spirit.

In a study conducted by Dr. Harold Stevenson, professor of psychology at the University of Michigan (in which he compared American schools to those in East Asia), the educational deficiencies of America's youth were traced to the motivational forces promoted by America's culture. In response to a "wish" question, Chicago children tended to wish for money and material objects, while Beijing children wished for educational goals.

Dr. Stevenson concluded that "clearly, a challenge in the U.S. is to create a greater cultural emphasis on education and academic success. But we must also make changes in the training of teachers and in their teaching schedules, so that they, too, will be able to incorporate sound teaching practices into their daily routines." So I ask you to take a moment to identify, refine and define your own brand of what "Authentic Guts," means to you.

Part I

High school graduation is always the goal for all of the Sankofa Scholars.

AUTHENTIC GUTS

Chapter 1

AUTHENTIC GUTS

> GOAL: The goal of Authentic Guts is to enhance the skills and knowledge of aspiring educators, parents and community stakeholders serving at risk youth using culturally relevant best practices.
>
> OBJECTIVES: By the end of this chapter the participants will be able to:
>
> - Describe *Authentic Guts and Grit*.
> - Define the meaning of "at risk."
> - Discuss the implications of knowing the value of self-knowledge in order to teach.

Fifteen years of new programs, testing, standards, and accountability have not ended racial achievement gaps in the United States (Sparks, 2016). The Coleman Report mandated by the Civil Rights Act of 1964, written by James Coleman found the average Black 12th grader in rural south registered an achievement level that was compared to that of a White 7th grader in the urban Northeast (Camera, 2016).

Do you know what grit means? No, not the ones you eat for breakfast with cheese and cajun shrimps in New Orleans. In terms of behavior, it's the courage and resolve of a persons character. It's the firmness and strength of their character. It's having an indomitable spirit. It's having the "guts" to be extraordinary successful and persevere through trials and tribulations. You have to know who you are as a person in order to reach children, especially children of different cultures. So who are you?

AUTHENTIC GUTS
Culturally Relevant Best Practices For Reaching The Youth 'At Risk"

CONNECTING WITH YOUR STUDENTS STARTS WITH YOU!

April Jones - Executive Director

The purpose of Authentic Guts is to highlight African-centered pedagogy, also a form of cultural resistance to dominant schooling practices that damage Black children's spirits and self-identities as an appropriate educational intervention in closing the achievement gap between Black and White students (Lee and Lomotey, 1990). African-Centered Thought (ACT) "is above all the total use of a method to effect psychological, political, social, cultural, and economic change." This happens "when the person become totally changed to a conscious level of involvement in his or her own liberation" (Asante, 1980 p. 56). African-centered education represent the empowerment of the Black family and thus it's children utilizing conscientization through education, transformation through ancient ecological and spiritual development, and self-actualization through economic and cultural independence. Culturally relevant education enhances the development of responsible adults in families and empower them to leave a legacy of talents, economic and academic skills to their children (Rivers, 1995).

An optimal culturally relevant education grounded in the African social ethics of Maat (balance, truth, justice, harmony) and the need for continuous personal study are necessary to facilitate the re-awakening process of self consciousness. Do you really know who you are? Do you really know where you are going? Do you have authentic guts and grit to do the important cultural work for not only our students, but for yourself?

> CONSCIENTIZATION IS A NEOLOGISM, COMING FROM THE SPANISH WORD CONSCIENTIZACIÓN. IT CONVEYS THE IDEA OF DEVELOPING, STRENGTHENING, AND CHANGING CONSCIOUSNESS. IT WAS CREATED IN THE FIELD OF EDUCATION, SPECIFICALLY OF ADULT EDUCATION, IN THE EARLY 1960S, PRODUCING AT THE SAME TIME A NEW CONCEPTION OF CONSCIOUSNESS.
> -*MARITZA MONTERO*

WHAT IS "AT RISK?"

"As education researcher Gloria Ladson-Billings once said of the term "at-risk," "We cannot saddle these babies at kindergarten with this label and expect them to proudly wear it for the next 13 years, and think, 'Well, gee, I don't know why they aren't doing good.'"

"At risk" for what is what a Black parent asked me one day at my former non-profit headquarters. She walked into my achievement center with her husband and their 10 year old son. She asked me if all the children enrolled in my summer program were Black? I told her no, we have students of all backgrounds that may have some troubles that classify them as being at risk. She didn't like the phrase *at risk*. I believe she felt that her son didn't belong in that category.

After introducing myself as a doctoral student at the local university, I went further to explain not only was I the executive director and founder of this non-profit, I was a prior military veteran, a resigned school teacher and at the age of 33, I too was considered an at risk youth. I told her I came from a single parent household and that alone put me in the category according to statistics. I was considered an at-risk youth because I was raised in the inner city of Chicago where drugs, violence, crime and murder prevailed. Needless to say that she did not enroll her son into my program. I heard a parent ask one day what the youth at-risk are at-risk for? Then she begin talking about her 15 year old son who had been fighting at school, smoking marijuana, in and out of juvenile justice departments and feeling suicidal. She said she wanted to learn more information about my nonprofit organization, Sankofa Achievement Center, Inc. Not only did I send her to the website and my email address, I told her that her son is at risk for going to jail, committing suicide, dropping out of high-school and not becoming a productive well rounded citizen if he continues down this road.

Valerie Strauss is an education writer who authors The Answer Sheet blog. She went to The Washington Post as an assistant foreign editor for Asia in 1987 and weekend foreign desk editor after working for Reuters as national security editor and a military/foreign affairs reporter on Capitol Hill. She also previously worked at UPI and the LA Times. She writes, "according to the Glossary of Education Reform, children are categorized in many ways — and being labeled "at-risk" is one of the most common in the educational context. What does it mean? Too much and, therefore, not much."

The term at-risk is often used to describe students or groups of students who are considered to have a higher probability of failing academically or dropping out of school. The term may be applied to students who face circumstances that could jeopardize their ability to complete school, such as homelessness, incarceration, teenage pregnancy, serious health issues, domestic violence, transiency (as in the case of migrant-worker families), or other conditions, or it may refer to learning disabilities, low test scores, disciplinary problems, grade retentions, or other learning-related factors that could adversely affect the educational performance and attainment of some students.

While educators often use the term at-risk to refer to general populations or categories of students, they may also apply the term to individual students who have raised concerns—based on specific behaviors observed over time—that indicate they are more likely to fail or drop out.

AUTHENTIC GUTS

"Her (Dr. Gloria Ladson-Billings) statement is very valid, but does it also help to know that there are factors that make certain kids more "vulnerable?"
-Durk Brown

Durk and I were in the curriculum and instruction graduate teaching program together at Tennessee State University. During his student teaching, he described how the experience of teaching was not what he thought it would be. He spent more time telling students to sit down and behave with little support from administration. He quit the profession before he got started.

When the term is used in educational contexts without qualification, specific examples, or additional explanation, it may be difficult to determine precisely what "at-risk" is referring to. In fact, "at-risk" can encompass so many possible characteristics and conditions that the term, if left undefined, could be rendered effectively meaningless. Still, kids are categorized as "at-risk" every day.

Here's a post on why that needs to stop.

Ivory A. Toldson, professor of counseling psychology at Howard University, editor in chief of the Journal of Negro Education, and president and chief executive of the QEM Network, a nonprofit organization in Washington dedicated to improving education from underrepresented students across the nation.

He was appointed by President Barack Obama as the executive director of the White House Initiative on Historically Black Colleges and Universities, which was tasked with devising strategies to booster federal support of HBCUs. And he has served as a senior research analyst for the Congressional Black Caucus Foundation on historically black colleges and universities.

Toldson writes "of all the terms used to describe students who don't perform well in traditional educational settings, few are used as frequently — or as casually — as the term "at-risk." The term is regularly used in federal and state education policy discussions, as well as popular news articles and specialty trade journals. It is often applied to large groups of students with little regard for the stigmatizing effect that it can have on students.

His most recent encounter with the term "at-risk" came after being tapped to review and critique a draft report for the Maryland Commission on Innovation and Excellence in Education, also known as the Kirwan Commission.

The Kirwan Commission, chaired by William E. Kirwan, a longtime higher education leader, was created in 2016 to make recommendations for improving education in Maryland. The initial draft of the Kirwan Commission report included a working group report called "More Resources for At-Risk Students."

Fortunately, in this instance, commission members were aware of some common objections to using "at-risk" to categorize students and publicly discussed the limitations of using the term. Some of those objections included risk of social stigma to students and lack of a uniform definition of "at-risk." However, when it came to finding a better way to describe students who show lower levels of academic success because of nonacademic factors, such as poverty, trauma and lack of English proficiency, commission members were not sure what term to use.

As an outside consultant for the commission, he was asked to come up with an acceptable alternative word or phrase. As he argues in his book, "No BS (Bad Stats): Black People Need People Who Believe in Black People Enough Not to Believe Every Bad Thing They Hear about Black People," three things are essential to good decision-making in education: good data, thoughtful analysis and compassionate understanding. What he says about the term "at-risk" is based on those three things.

Practical uses exist

First, he acknowledges that, paired with good data, "at-risk" is practically useful and generally accepted in professional and academic settings. Used effectively, identifying risk and protective factors can help mitigate harm to students. For example, dating back to the 1960s, research about how exposure to lead placed children at risk for cognitive impairments helped educators create safer learning environments for students by removing lead from paint, toys and drinking water. Today, in educational research and practice, educators routinely use "at-risk" to classify students who do not perform well in traditional educational settings. However, the factors that determine "at-risk" are often either unknown or beyond the control of the student, caregiver or educational provider.

As a scholar of counseling psychology — and as one who specializes in counseling persons of black African ancestry — he believes that to designate a child "at-risk" for factors such as growing up in a single-parent household, having a history of abuse or neglect, how much money their families make, or their race or ethnicity adds more chaos and confusion to the situation. Instead, compassion and care are what are needed, according to Toldson.

Never use 'at-risk' as an adjective

Using "at-risk" as an adjective for students is problematic. It makes "at-risk" a category like honors student, student athlete or college-bound student. "Risk" should describe a condition or situation, not a person. Therefore, "More Resources for At-Risk Students" might more appropriately be "More Resources to Reduce Risk Factors for Students."

Be specific

Assessments of risk should be based on good data and thoughtful analysis — not a catch-all phrase to describe a cluster of ill-defined conditions or characteristics. If the phrase "at-risk" must be used, it should be in a sentence such as: " 'This' places students at risk for 'that.' " If the "this" and "that" are not clearly defined, the "at-risk" characterization is useless at best, and harmful at worst. But when these variables are clearly defined, it better enables educators and others to come up with the solutions needed to reduce specific risk factors and improve outcomes.

Skip the alternatives

Common alternatives to "at-risk" include "historically underserved," "disenfranchised" and "placed at-risk." These indicators acknowledge that outside forces have either not served the individual student or population well, or have assigned the at-risk label to unwitting subjects. These phrases move the conversation in the right direction. However, using these phrases still comes up short because they obscure the problem. For example, research suggests that child abuse, poverty and racism can place students at risk. However, different strategies can lessen each risk. When the risk factors are more clearly identified, it puts educators and others in a better position to strategically confront the issues that impede student learning. It also better enables educators and others to view the individual student separately and apart from the particular risk.

Some have suggested replacing the term "at-risk" with "at-promise." While well-intended, the problem I see with that is it could easily be seen as a condescending euphemism for the term it was meant to replace. The best alternative for 'at-risk'

In his book, he describe an in-service training for staff members of a public high school, in which he asked the participants to describe the neighborhoods of their students. He heard phrases such as "crime-ridden," "broken homes" and "drug-infested." He then asked if anyone grew up in neighborhoods that had similar characteristics. After several raised their hands, he asked, "How did you grow up in such a neighborhood and still become successful?" This question spurred a more meaningful discussion about the neighborhoods where students are from. It was a discussion that considered community assets — such as hope and resilience — against a more thoughtful examination of community challenges.

Every student has a combination of risk and protective factors among their friends, in their homes, schools and neighborhoods. These factors can help or hurt their academic potential. Students who live in poverty, or have been assigned to special education, or have a history of trauma, or who are English learners may or may not be "at risk" depending on their respective protective factors. But, when students are labeled "at-risk," it serves to treat them as a problem because of their risk factors.

Instead, students' unique experiences and perspectives should be normalized, not marginalized. This reduces a problem known as "stereotype threat," a phenomenon in which students perform worse academically when they are worried about living up to a negative stereotype about their group. For all these reasons and more, he believes the best alternative to describe "at-risk students" is simply "students." For what it's worth, the Kirwan Commission agrees. The commission recently revised its call for "More Resources for At-Risk Students" to "More Resources to Ensure All Students are Successful."

Engaging youth can be either meaningful or meaningless, effective or ineffective, positive or negative, and constructive or destructive, depending on how or in what ways youth are engaged in an activity. Young people today face many challenges. These challenges include changes in family support structures, unsettled social norms and marginalization by service providers and policy makers. Young people who have difficulty coping with stressors of life often lack motivation, confidence, and have low self-esteem. These alienated feelings often lead to "at risk" behaviors deemed "high risk" by society. Some examples of such behaviors are substance abuse, sexual promiscuity and low school performance or even worse school drop-out.

The term "at risk" youth has different meanings; however, within the context of Authentic Guts, this term references youth susceptible to poverty, homelessness, abusive/addictive behaviors, mental health challenges, discrimination, stigma, and/or compromised developmental outcomes.

Action Item 1

Challenge

Define the term "at risk" and make a list of expectations for connecting with students through self-knowledge with reference to the terms Authentic Guts and Grit applicable inside and out the classroom.

Chapter 2
Personal To Practice

> OBJECTIVES: By the end of this chapter the participants will be able to:
>
> - Consider "current events " in relation to our youth and reaching them.
> - Review and evaluate personal experiences for effective teaching.
> - Analyze the effectiveness of self-coping as a teaching technique.

Danquan asked if he could stay in my classroom with me during lunch time. I told him sure as I lined the students up for lunch. I waited in the cafeteria for Danquan to walk through the lunch line to get his tray of food. We walked back to my classroom and I began scrolling through my emails as I sat at the desk. Danquan sat at his desk eating his food. After a few minutes, Danquan said "Ms. Jones, can I tell you something," I said sure. He goes on to tell me that he had a gun that he sits on the air conditioning unit outside his bedroom window for protection. This is a 7th grade student, living in city housing and his 16 year old sister was just murdered to senseless gun violence. He walks to school everyday alone and feels like he is at war on a daily basis. How would you respond as a teacher? Can you relate to this student? If not, then how can you?

Preparing my speech for the candlelight vigil, thinking about Danquan and his family in tears, where do we go from here?

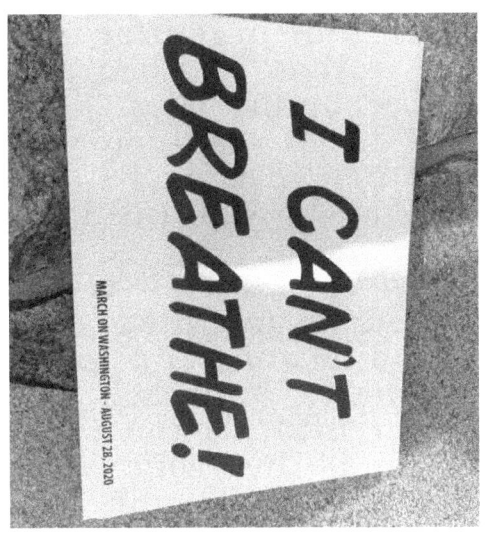

Black Girls Ride to the March On Washington

2020 Washington D.C.

The newspaper headlines read

"Zimmerman aquitted in Treyvon Martin Case,

"Mike Brown had marijuana in his system."

How can we expect our youth to focus enough at home and/or school, pass standardized testing, and pay attention to their teachers when they are witnessing police brutality on a daily basis? Our children are scared. Parents are frightened to send their children to school. Black children are being shot dead like dogs in the street by the hands of police. Even worse is same race violence.

I'm very upset with my current situation and the situation of many other African American, Black, Hispanic, interracial, same-sex, immigrant and or refugee person with the ways in which we are being treated currently in the United States of America. During a time where an African American President has sat in the White House.

We would have thought we have overcame the stereotypical, systematic and blatant racism in America by now. The lately newspaper headlines have read "Zimmerman acquitted in Treyvon Martin Case, "Mike Brown had marijuana in his system." Breonna Taylor shot dead while sleeping, Philando Castile, Sandra Bland and the countless others killed unjustifiably. Say their names.

We would think racial and social justice inequities had become a thing of the past. The system is designed with a prison pipeline directly from school to the prison cell. If students are not meeting the basic reading level according to standardized testing by the third grade, then a prison cell is being built for that person.

The research findings has shown, if a child can't read by the third grade, then that child is more than likely going to end up dead or incarcerated.

AUTHENTIC GUTS

PERSONAL TO PRACTICE

In "Per Aa Asa Hilliard: The Great House of Black Light for Educational Excellence," an article published shortly after Asa Hilliard made his transition to the ancestors, Nobles (2008) states "To only quote Asa or debate about what he stood for would fail to fully honor his life" (p. 743). While Nobles understands that the written and spoken word are viable means through which ideas are transmitted, he cautions about the tendency among intellectuals to engage in academic discourse that is not practical.

The work involved in "doing Asa" (Nobles, 2008) and actualizing Hilliard's (2002) pedagogy requires tapping into ancient and formal sources of cultural information; reading oral histories from elders; studying personal accounts written by or about Africans who have been through socialization systems; and participation in some form of African derived socialization system. Hilliard advocated for African agency and advised "No one will do the important cultural work for us. We must do it for ourselves" (p. 115).

It is this sense of urgent agency formation that illustrates Hilliard's commitment to developing an African-centered pedagogy that can assist in facilitating a re-Africanization process.

Culturally Relevant Pedagogy (CRP) is a philosophical outlook towards one's approach to teaching that informs the what, the how, and the why. CRP focuses on the academic and personal success of students as individuals and as a collective. It ensures students engage in academically rigorous curriculum and learning, feel affirmed in their identities and experiences, and develop the knowledge and skills to engage the world and others critically.

CRP, a pedagogical framework coined by Dr. Gloria Ladson-Billings in the early '90s, rests on three fundamental pillars—academic achievement, cultural competence, and sociopolitical consciousness. These three pillars work in tandem with one another—in other words, a culturally relevant teacher cannot focus on one pillar without also inherently focusing on the others.

Deberianah Begley's brother Danquan and mother Tika Begley comfort each other as a crowd gathers for a candlelight vigil at the James Cayce Public Housing Development in Nashville, Tenn., Monday, Oct 9, 2017.
Lacy Atkins/The Tennessean

PERSONAL TO PRACTICE

The younger Clardy's & The older Clardy's Excelling Academically as a family.

Because of miseducation, people of African descent throughout the African diaspora have been taught to view themselves through a Eurocentric lens. One of the primary ways the Eurocentric lens maintains and perpetuates cultural hegemony is by promoting European history and culture as superior while degrading and devaluing anything associated with Africa and people of African descent.

Such miseducation and Eurocentric cultural socialization processes have caused many people of African descent to internalize anti-African ideas. Asa Hilliard, also known as Nana Baffour Amankwatia II, addresses this cultural disconnect. He called diasporian people to study African indigenous traditions, to counter cultural denigration, and to reconstruct African indigenous socialization systems.

As an act of cultural decolonization (Nobles, 2018), Hilliard's involvement in re-conceptualizing and re-Africanizing the educational process of African Americans serves as an example of an African-centered praxis that can be used to improve the educational potential and educational possibilities of African people.

Sankofa Campers engaged in communication activties

Blacks, since the 1700s have structured and organized independent schools to provide cultural and intellectual needs for their children (Ratteray & Shujaa, 1987). By the end of the nineteenth century, Black independent schools were taken over by public schools. The outcome allowed for the masses of Black people during the 1990s to be schooled in American public schools, furthermore, allowing conditioning in the thought and reality of European culture
(Ratteray & Shujaa, 1987; Woodson, 1990).

Many of the traditional schools including Historically Black College and Universities, from daycares, preschools-12 grades, and higher education all follow a European curriculum and standard. Any school that has a majority Black and/or Latino student population with an administration and faculty of majority Black or Latino all follow a European culture, because they must adhere to policies, standards, and values that are not culturally or historically relevant to their students.

The Black administration and faculty are not in control of their student's education, it is decided for them. From the scholarship of educational scholars, have contended that these complications for education were done purposely to exploit, alienate and discriminate the masses of Black people so cultural and intellectual liberation would not manifest (Freire, 1973, Hillard, 1998; King, 1991; Woodson, 1990).

"AFTER FILLING OUT QUESTIONNAIRES AND BEING EXAMINED IT WAS SUGGESTED I PLACE HIM ON MEDICATION"
FAATYMAH KITT

PERSONAL TO PRACTICE

The prominent educational leader Carter G. Woodson (1990) contested that Black children were being held back to reach their full capabilities due to the schools secluding them from African culture and traditions and idolizing European culture. The trends among some of the urban charter schools are having high test scores and very high suspension rates. In order to help improve charter schools, there should be a focus on the underfunding of the school and salary of the teachers. Some urban chartered schools due to being underfunded miss the social component of school activities such as homecoming. The marginalized students are being trained to follow instructions and think little. There must be a change of narrative on how marginalized students are educated.

The paradigm of education in urban charter schools has gradually switched to focusing on schooling and less on education. To reform this system and structure, the institution itself must be dismantled and replaced with educationally-cultured policies.

Institutional racism, micro-aggression, surveillance, and physical conformity must be replaced with a pedagogy or a paradigm shift of cultural metaphor style of teaching. In the school and classroom setting, factors that must be examined are cultural, structural, racial, and identity variables. This would also assist in helping the students excel academically and deter bad behavior. The zero-tolerance and no excuse policies need to be dismantled and revised without bias and include a culturally relevant clause. In turn, this shift of handling the marginalized students would decrease the number of suspensions and expulsions and increase the number of graduations.

As quoted by Molefi K. Asante, "You cannot leave the education of your children simply to those whose purposes are different from your own and expect the children to grow up and follow the path of the ancestors." The African Centered Movement had its early beginnings in the 1700s with the Black independent schools. The parents during the moment strongly insisted on controlling public schools or forming independent institutions going beyond the public structures (Ratteray & Shujaa, 1987).

As the efforts grew, the movement was called Independent African Centered School Movement, which was based on promoting academic excellence, embedded with cultural relevance and character development (Lee, 1992). The movement came back due to the failure of public education for Black students and the augment of international movement for pan-African unity (Giddings, 2001). In order to achieve the success of African Centered Thought in the classroom and curriculum, faculty and administration must focus on reclaiming and reteaching African history to the young Black scholars. Also, centered around African education, creativity with art and spiritual growth should be included in the classroom and curriculum. The schools, administration, faculty, professors, and teachers that educate Black minds must focus on the rebuilding and reforming of African civilization through their scholarly work and pedagogy.

These educational institutions should repair and construct African history and its culture. The creation and continuation of ACT in educational institutions will help to continue the legacy of the African people. These institutions that implement ACT would serve as a safe space to preserve and continue the work started by black scholars. The history of the African people which is lost or not told has a space to which the African history can be told truthfully by African people.

African centered thought essentially says that there must be an understanding of pre-colonial education in Africa, to explain the value of education to people of African descent. The history of education for people of African descent must be investigated for the community to fully grasp the struggles and obstacles experienced by their ancestors regarding obtaining knowledge and higher learning. The thought also emphasizes the removal of European standards to replace it with the standards of African people. Africanization is the process of celebrating, embracing and preserving the culture and history of African people.

The Critical Race Theory framework helps to show how the American educational system was not created with the student of color in mind but steeped in a foundation built on Eurocentric values and concerns. The theory examines the issues of race and class, but not culture. Culture is an important aspect to consider for a group of people, because examining the culture one can understand customs, arts, social institutions, and achievements; their way of life, thinking, beliefs, and behaving.

There is a difference between schooling and education. According to Shujaa Mwalimu, schooling is defined as instruction in school. Mwalimu defined education as both the gaining of knowledge and development of character. Education happens inside and outside of the classroom. Schooling promotes alienation, discrimination, and exploitation, which does not allow for a just and safe environment. As a result, the educational needs and experiences of students of color have been largely ignored and the policies have had a negative impact on their communities. Education is the priority over schooling, it is a life-long process (Mwalimu, 1993).

> *I used to be chubby when I was younger, but working out in the early mornings with Camp Imani helped me realize my physical potential and started me on my journey to slimming up and playing on my high school football team. Thank you!*
> *Theodore (TJ)*

PERSONAL TO PRACTICE

It is critical that scholars in education move from conceptual confusion to conceptual clarity (Hilliard, 1995). A key feature of Hilliard's work centers on constructing an appropriate conceptual framework from which to grapple with the education of African . Americans. An appropriate framework is needed to break through the ideological barriers and conceptual constraints that prevent educators from properly understanding issues.

Within this context, Hilliard (1995) discusses how conceptual confusion is often a consequence of misconstruing the problem through euphemistic labeling. Euphemistic labeling limits discussions about educational disparities by utilizing milder sounding words like race relations, intergroup relations, multiculturalism,
and diversity (Hilliard, 1995).

These terms operate as euphemisms
that obscure the core concepts and issues that need to be addressed and contribute
to creating more conceptual confusion. By eliminating euphemisms, the hard and often uncomfortable questions about the relationship between education and culture can be asked. For example, who are the powerful and privileged? What role does education play in their obtaining and maintaining their powerful position over the oppressed? What is White supremacy and
how does it benefit from African American children receiving an inferior education? What type of cultural education is needed to counter White supremacy?

Stating educational issues in terms of power, privilege, oppression, and White supremacy changes the content and substance of the discourse by using transparent nomenclature that allows for conceptual clarity about disparities in education (Hilliard, 1995).

Bethea (2018) demonstrates how African-centered pedagogical approaches can be used in college classrooms to create knowledge, foster learning, nurture creativity, enhance mastery of skill, and encourage social action, transformation, and healing.

Goals of African-centered pedagogy:

(a) legitimize African epistemology;
(b) advance productive community and cultural practices;
(c) extend and build
upon the indigenous language;
(d) reinforce community ties and service to family, community, nation, race, and world;
and (e) promote positive social
relationships.

Be Diliglent in the pursuit of teaching

PERSONAL TO PRACTICE

I struggled with bullyism during elementary school because of an infiltrated tissue scar on my arm.
Dr. April. A. Jones

One sunny day while teaching 9th grade, I decided it was a great day to put my students in a morning meeting circle outside in the grass before starting my lesson. Each morning we shared something with each other during the morning meeting. I tried to mimic a socratic seminar with my students daily offering an organized social experience and it also helped them with their communication skills. This also created and set the culture, climate and tone in the classroom. All students knew all were welcomed, respected and creativity encouraged.

There was always a talking piece. It could be any object that only the speaker holds and all other students in the circle knew to be quiet and listen to the speaker. One student shared her excitement about her family weekend at the water park. When my turn came, I shared my personal incident about my infiltrated arm. The conversation object was passed to Jeremy who was wearing a t-shirt and some jeans. The other students had on shorts and sandals. It was panning out to be a hot day in Nashville. Jeremy shared that he never has been to a water park before because he doesn't like to take his pants off. He said his leg was caught on fire while trying to rob rival gang members in a drug house and the scar from the third degree burns were ugly. This gave me a teachable moment to connect with Jeremy about how I felt and still feel about my scar. I told him I could relate to him and that it was nothing to be ashamed of. I encouraged him to show his scar when he was ready. Other students started to chime in about scars and incidents. We could've talked for hours about that subject. The next day, Jeremy wore shorts! Some students asked to touch my arm and Jeremy's leg. We connected and was able to move forward in learning.

My high school was predominately caucasian. I didn't want to lose my African foundations. There is a stigma in the black community that when you go away to school in a different environment you are considered an "uncle tom, a sell-out," you are betraying your own kind. *Acting* white as I have heard many times. So while in high school I began researching more about my own culture.

I learned about African centered curriculums and realized although my elementary school was not labeled African centered, the education I received, how I perceived it, what my teachers told me on and off the record and how they helped motivate me as an adult; I had indeed received an African centered education.

Because of the enrichment I received, I began to love to read at an early age, setting goals and reaching them and being celebrated from doing such.

I knew my family had a rich heritage of being well-rounded and successful, I mean my last name is Jones, lol. Digging deeply into my past gave me an enormous sense of pride, self-esteem, and self-motivation. How can we give our students these feelings when we are not related to them? Sometimes children spend more hours during the day with their teachers and mentors than their working parents.

So as educators and mentors, we have to be able to connect with our students. This is how we bring those feelings to life for them. And remember I mentioned earlier, connecting with students begins with you.

I had determination molded in me, instilled in me and embedded in me. When I went to face the ills of society which seldom fell upon me in my lifetime, I was able to keep my head up and walk forward continuing to seek wisdom and reach for the same stars my ancestors reached for.

The recognition of my hard work was a self-fulfilling reward that continues to drive cultural excellence in all I do. My students that I cross on a daily basis often are empty and in absence of this type of effective practice.

The Fear of the Creator, fear of my mother and the fear of failure gave me intuitive motivation to learn deeply and study hard. In this studying I found that my theory on African centered education plays an important role in the holistic education of at-risk students.

I am a direct bi-product of that. In my research from high school until the present I have gathered my teaching style and philosophy from many controversial educational theorists. I will discuss these theorists further in the chapter four.

One night while lesson planning, I took a break to browse my Facebook page. I saw in my newsfeed where a little 9 year old boy was caught on camera slapping the shit out of his drug overdosed mother. He was yelling wake up! Can you talk to me? Say something! Yelling at the top of his lungs as he once again slaps the shit out of her over and over again. Now the caption of this video said "when your mother is too high to talk". Now I do believe this little boy being raised in this environment would put him at risk for several behaviors deemed at risk by society. So how can we help him, when he comes to school disheveled without a pencil and he is hungry? Do we expect him to pay attention, focus and be the best student he can be?

I have had to pull from my resources of life experiences in order to make connections with my students. I've been to jail, I've been in a single parent home, we had government cheese, food stamps and I remember eating sugar sandwiches at times when we didn't have much food. I knew how important it was for me to eat free breakfast, free lunch during school and the free after school meal. Feeding programs are vital to our low socio-economic communities and at-risk families.

SAC Scholars hanging out and staying out of trouble.

Teaching has become an incredible task to bare. Having resigned from my city's public school system twice, I witnessed countless of my colleagues leave the teaching field even before finishing their student teaching. I have had many people, family and close friends alert me to the fact that I am probably making a big mistake leaving the classroom.

My desire to help our youth is so strong. I could not teach inside the four walls. I needed a creative way to break the walls down and really teach our youth. You need authentic guts as I mentioned earlier to face the myriad of challenges our youths face today. The politics of the school building sometimes doesn't allow for creativeness; or shall I say, realness. The realness we need to really make a difference in a child's life. Our students need to feel the connection.

Action Item 2

Reflect

Reflect on things you have had to cope with as an adult. What was the event and what technique did you use? How can you use this technique in your own teaching practices?

Think back on both the current events of today and past experiences. How can we build upon these experiences to connect with our children and students?

Part II

BEST PRACTICES FOR ALL STUDENTS

Ya'Mar is a Sankofa Scholar. This picture is of him graduating from 8th grade.

Chapter 3
EDUCATION

> OBJECTIVES: By the end of this chapter the reader will be able to:
>
> - Discuss and interpret the perceptions of African Centered Curriculums and the impact on school programs.
> - Review and evaluate Holistic teaching approaches.
> - Analyze stereotypes and children's self-perception in relation to their race.

I have felt how it is to sit in a classroom where you are the only person that looks like you. When Igor, my second grader from Croatia told me he felt by himself at school because there were no other Croatian students at our school, I was able to relate to him because I have been in conference rooms where I was the only black person at the table feeling alone. I was put on the spot during this conference. Being asked multiple direct questions on my skill and knowledge during board meetings made me feel singled out. No child should ever feel singled out, or made feel insecure. I use all of my different life moments as a suitcase of tools I can pull out the bag later to use them for connecting in an endearing, but firm way with my students.

When I think of my educational theory as I have developed into my role as a community advocate and educational leader, I often reflect how my personal educational theory has derived. I remember life lesson conversations as I rode to and from school with Ms. Purnell and Mrs. Vines. During the gentrification of Bronzeville the 3 flat apartment we lived at on Greenwood street was sold and purchased by an affluent Black family. My mother nor my teachers wanted me to switch schools. The attachment to the school and community was so holistic. Ms. Purnell agreed to pick me up and drop me off on her route to work. Mrs. Vines and Ms. Purnell came to pick me up for school. We all rode to school and I learned from them not only in the classroom, but during those 30 min daily drives. They were an extension of my mother because it takes a strong village.

I think about all of the literature, journals and other pieces of informative educational materials I have read throughout my educational career. The combination of my past experiences and researching have helped me form a critical analyses of education. Let's talk about some of the past theorist who have come before me and drove my belief in cultural relevant teaching. Propelled me to from learning to teaching using the foundation of African-centered curriculums to develop student pride. Students need the feeling of pride to push for personal excellence in everything they do.

Afterschool music lesson with Mr. Stefan Forbus

" WE SHOULD START ENCOURAGING THE RIGHT MINDSET INSTEAD OF SIMPLY TELLING STUDENTS WHAT TO DO.

I have been inspired by philosophers and theorists who were labeled for their "radical" separatist perspectives of education on the black community (i.e. Booker T. Washington, W.E.B. Dubois, Malcolm X and Martin Luther King, Jr. or Marcus Garvey). Each one of those scholars that I mentioned whose philosophies inspired part of the development of my education theory, were simultaneously fighting for injustices and inequalities. They had either a right wing way or a left wing way of obtaining their goals.

Booker T. Washington called for Blacks to 'the accepting of discrimination' for that time being and rather focus on elevating themselves through hard work and economic gain in order to win the respect of whites.

W.E.B. Du Bois, and his 1903 radical theory against Booker T. Washington in his famous book *The Souls Of Black Folk* where he charged that Washington's strategy kept the Black man down rather than freed him.

Martin Luther King, Jr. wanted non-violence amidst the face of oppression to overcome inequities of black people. Malcolm X said "by any means necessary" for black people to defend themselves against inequities and unequal rights, crystallizing his radical theories against Martin Luther King Jr.

My educational theory and practice has been built on the shoulders of those who have paved the way for me, before me and impacted the educational world for our communities in our present day society.

My belief in the Creator, my personal life experiences, attainment of higher education, and social and emotional learning environments helped shaped my current philosophies in education.

The orginal Sankofa Headquarters and first year of Camp

With her mother not around and father incarcerated, her Grandmother has always kept her active and engaged. We have a large population of grandparents raising our youth today.

"

IT IS A VERY URBAN ART FORM, MOST LIKELY TO BE ABOUT THE AFRICAN AMERICAN EXPERIENCE, BUT NOT ALWAYS, AND EXACTLY WHAT THESE KIDS NEED- THE OPPORTUNITY TO EXPRESS THEMSELVES IN A SAFE, ACCEPTING ENVIRONMENT.

Pat Blankenship

I remember sitting in my fifth grade classroom at Florence B. Price Elementary School in 1992. This would be the same year my little brother was born. My family decided to name him Jawanza Oboi Jones after the respected and honored Dr. Jawanza Kunjufu.

I learned at a very young age about the deep rooted philosophies of Dr. Kunjufu. Dr. Kunjufu had visited my elementary school and gave a life changing motivational speech on the topic of education and why education was so important, especially for us in the Black community.

With my older brother and my mother being very familiar with the teachings of Dr. Kunjufu, it was a no brainer that we would name the youngest of my mother's four children, her second son, Jawanza. I can recall sitting in the living room excited to tell my family about the speech I heard from the day at school and discussing as a family Dr. Kunjufu's ideologies together.

There has always been a connection that was made academically for me between my home life conversations. My family conversations implored the feeling that I was a valuable member of my family, school and community despite the fact I was the youngest at the time. The education I received during my elementary school years immersed me in a holistic education. The teachers at Price Elementary engaged me, challenged me and cared for me. My development of self-esteem and motivation to succeed was magnified through the teaching and learning experiences I had received. I knew I wanted to be an advocate for justice and excel in education just as those who have paved the way for me had done.

During my K-8 public schooling at Price, I was exposed to an African-Centered education. Although the school was not labeled such, the teachers Freeman, Bull, Stein, Candia, Lott, Vines, Purnell, and St. Leger all played a part in my growth and development.

I think it is absolute power in the fact that I can still remember each one of my elementary school teachers' names and their ultimate effect upon me. Some of those lessons whether positive or negative impacted me. Moreover, I don't remember any of my highschool teachers except for maybe 3 out of 20 of them. I can only recall 1 of my college undergraduate professors. Through graduate studies and four different universities I can remember a handful of professors.

The only school that had an African Centered Curriculum model is the one and only school I attended in K-8. It produced a confidant and intuitive motivated young lady. It created and gave all students a chance to succeed, with a strong caring push.

It really qualified as a holistic (well-rounded) education. I was saddened to hear of the school closing down years ago. The community of teachers and the culture and climate of the school all were allowing me to know who I am and where I came from and which direction I should be heading.

Hands on learning during Camp Imani summer camp program (Teachable moments have to be capitalized on immediately.

AUTHENTIC GUTS

EDUCATION CONT.

Theorist from the past driving the future

In this section I would like to introduce a few theorists that have shaped my thinking for teaching.

Dr. Jacob Hudson Carruthers, founding member of the Association for the Study of Classical African Civilizations (ASCAC) was a prolific deep thinker, researcher, author, scholar, educator and master teacher. He maintained leadership involvement in the national African Centered Education Movement.

With Dr. Carruthers' leadership, a global research project was established. Heading The African World History Project, being a founding member of the Kemetic Institute, Dr. Carruthers developed and remained dedicated to the research, rescue and restoration of classical African antiquity, Nile Valley civilizations and the study of ancient Kemetic (African) cultures.

Dr. Carruthers theory in the direct study and interpretation of the indigenous language used in ancient Kemet (Africa) was the key to understanding their logic and thinking.

Rather than referring and depending on existing translations done by western Egyptologists, Dr. Carruthers traveled back and forth to Egypt for the purposes of transferring and translating the writings on the temple walls and reading directly from the rock to develop a true African Centered epistemology. He had a desire to have a better understanding of African history and capture the wisdom and thinking of the ancestors.

Dr. Wade Nobles is a master teacher, psychologist, Kemetologist, professor, Jega, Sage and deep thinker. He is a professor in the Department of African Studies at San Francisco State University. Dr. Nobles is also the founder and executive director of the Institute for The Advanced Study of Black Family, Life and Culture. Dr. Nobles is well respected and has impacted the black community nationally and internationally for his research and scholarship.

Camp Imani 2013 at Coleman Community Center

Jefferson Street SAC Headquarters

AUTHENTIC GUTS

EDUCATION CONT.

Students team building after conflict resolution

" "THE PROBLEM OF THE TWENTIETH CENTURY IS THE PROBLEM OF THE COLOR-LINE."

W.E.B. DU BOIS

AUTHENTIC GUTS

As an African Centered psychologist and educator, Dr. Noble's contemporary educational theory views human development and social behaviors from an African Centered human development model of "Sun sum." The Sun Sum represents the spiritual orientation and affective processes of cultural cosmic life forces that flow through the embryonic fluids of ankh (life) and re-generated through "Nsake," the effect and affect of human connections.

With his deep study of indigenous African Centered traditions of teaching and learning, Dr. Nobles constructed educational best practices in African pedagogy using the "Nsake Sun Sum" model. Transforming human consciousness and behavior through culturally relevant methods of excellence in education.

William Edward Burghardt Du Bois was an American civil rights activist, leader, Pan-Africanist, sociologist, educator, historian, writer, editor, poet, and scholar. Du Bois, the first African American to receive a Ph.D. in the subject of history from Harvard University. He was a Pan Africanist, scholar as well as a Fisk University graduate.

W.E.B. Du Bois served as the voice in the black community. For many African Americans from 1910 through the 1930's. Du Bois continued to fight against the demand by many whites that Black education be "primarily industrial and that Black southern students learn to accept White supremacy."

The local community center allowed us to utilize the swimming pool during summer camp days - External Partnerships

Friendships that will last a lifetime

"
THE ROOTS OF EDUCATION ARE BITTER, BUT THE FRUIT IS SWEET. – ARISTOTLE

EDUCATION CONT.

He emphasized the great need for blacks to get a higher education. This education according to Du Bois would allow for the Black American to develop leadership capacity among the most able percent of Black Americans, who he referred to as "The Talented Ten".

In the 1930s, Du Bois penned articles that advocated voluntary segregation, maintaining that black children would receive a better education from black teachers.

I personally have always felt a connection when I was being taught by black teachers; negative and/or positive connections.

I remember taking a course at Chicago State University in African American History. The class was taught by a Chinese woman. I sat in that class thinking, she knows more than my own people know about their culture and history. At the same time, the lecture was cold and educational. I didn't feel the connection.

I also acknowledge educational theorists B.F. Skinner whose theory says: "instruction must be based on operant reinforcement in which sets of learners acts are reinforced or strengthened, so as to increase the probability of their reoccurrence in the future."

Friedrich Froebel whose learning by doing theory focused on the doctrines of free self-activity, creativeness, social participation and motor expression.

Edwin Thorndike's connectionism theory that produced the first scientific learning theory and is the starting point for any study of modern instructional technology "the best teacher uses books and appliances as well as his own insight, sympathy and magnetism,"

Some education theorists would critically analyze and/or oppose and reject my theory on the basis of it not being one hundred percent African Centered (built using an "All Black" foundation and structure). This rejection happens solely because I have non-African descent acknowledgement of educational theories.

Ms. Ari, Nashville local artist, engaging our scholars in music and theater

AUTHENTIC GUTS

EDUCATION CONT.

I hope my continued research on African centered curriculum models, and the implementations of this curriculum will reform the educational system in which I work and live in. Our low socioeconomic communities in which I have come from are being mis-educated, under-educated and our students are failing to receive a holistic education.

When Danquan approached my desk after school to tell me his sister was killed over the weekend in front of his house while they were celebrating his 14 birthday. His sister was innocently shot as she sat on the front porch of the birthday celebration. Two guys were running down the street shooting at one another. It is a war out in the streets for our youth. I didn't know how to make a connection with Danquan. I went back to a place where I was frightened and confused if I was to make a connection and be able to help my student. I remembered that day being on the plane headed to Afghanistan.

The pilot placed the internal lights from white to dim red lights. We had to fly around in the air for quite a little while to ensure we landed while it was dark. I'm sure a big US military plane landing in Afghanistan during broad day light was a sure target for a rocket. I use that experience as a young 19 year old soldier, that fear of the unknown to connect with Danquan in that moment.

The moment when the commanders and sergeants began sliding cans of ammunition down the aisles of the plane and told us to load up all six 30 round magazine clips, I was honestly scared. When they said move! move! move! - and we rushed off the plane in formation. I just knew a bomb was going to kill us all. I used those feelings to relate to my students who are constantly at fear in their communities for a multitude of reasons. Danquan received grief counseling, and found strength to move forward despite his trauma. With the help of counselors, through our school community external partners and extending an arm around his single mother, we were able to keep Danquan on track, engaged and excited to continue to live. Danquan is doing great in high school now.

My theory is that African centered education impacts the at-risk student holistically thereby producing successful, well-embodied capable citizens who have deep understanding of their culture and rich traditions.

A holistic education includes character education, mentorship, social and emotional learning whereby self-esteem, confidence and motivation is not a goal of education, but part of the pedagogy of culturally relevant excellence.

Keeping them active and engaged at Rocket Town

"THE LEARNING PROCESS CONTINUES UNTIL THE DAY YOU DIE."
– KIRK DOUGLAS

The children put raised garden beds behind their school and grew fruits and vegetables

AUTHENTIC GUTS

HOLISTIC EDUCATON

Summer Campers learn music

The purpose of holistic education is to prepare students to meet the challenges of living as well as academics. Holistic education believes it is important for young people to learn:

- About themselves
- About healthy relationships and pro-social behavior
- Social development
- Emotional development
- Resilience
- As well as to see beauty, have awe, experience transcendence, and appreciate some sense of "truths."

Consider your life's greatest challenges. What did you need to know to overcome the obstacles you faced? Consider your greatest successes. What did you need to know in order to achieve those successes? Then ask yourself, how many of those things that I needed to know did I learn in school?

For thousands of years before schools there were social groups which taught people about the great adventure of being human; its trials and tribulations, its challenges, and its enormous possibilities for human goodness and even greatness.

These groups were extended families, communities or tribes or clans, and religions. For the most part, these groups have disappeared or become compartmentalized in people's lives.

Now, it is predominantly popular culture (the media, music) and schools from which young people can learn about what it means to be human. But culture has it own agenda (not the welfare of children), and schools were not designed to replace extended families, communities, and religions.

They were designed to prepare people for the world of work; to give them the skill sets that would help them up the ladder of material success.

THE CLARK DOLL TEST

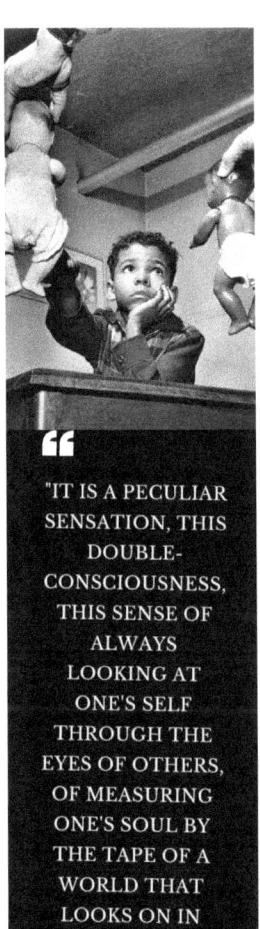

The Clark Doll test was conducted by Dr. Kenneth Clark and his wife Mamie Clark for her masters degree thesis. The study focused on stereotypes and children's self-perception in relation to their race. The results of Clarks study were used to prove that school segregation was distorting the minds of young black kids, causing them to internalize stereotypes and racism, to the point of making them hate themselves.

The Clark Doll Test is well known due to its social relevance and impact although some say that the results lack experimental weight. It found contrasts among children attending segregated schools in Washington, DC versus those in integrated schools in New York.

In 1954 in Brown v Board of Education, the experiment helped to persuade the American Supreme Court that separate but equal schools for blacks and whites were anything but equal in practice and is therefore illegal or against the law. This made the experiment even more controversial. It marked the beginning of the end of Jim Crow.

In the experiment, Clark showed black children with ages ranging from 6 to 9, two dolls, one white and the other black.

The following questions were asked in the order below-

Show me the doll that you like best or that you would like to play with.
Show me the doll that is the nice doll.
Show me the doll that looks bad;
Give me the doll that looks like a white child.
Give me the doll that looks like a colored child.
Give me the doll that looks like a Negro child.
Give me the doll that looks like you.

> "IT IS A PECULIAR SENSATION, THIS DOUBLE-CONSCIOUSNESS, THIS SENSE OF ALWAYS LOOKING AT ONE'S SELF THROUGH THE EYES OF OTHERS, OF MEASURING ONE'S SOUL BY THE TAPE OF A WORLD THAT LOOKS ON IN AMUSED CONTEMPT AND PITY.
>
> W.E.B. DU BOIS

We took the city bus to the museum at Camp Imani

AUTHENTIC GUTS

EDUCATION CONT.

The researchers found that black children often chose to play with the white dolls more than the black ones. When the kids were asked to fill in a human figure with the color of their own skin, they frequently chose a lighter shade than their actual skin color. The children also gave the color white positive attributes like good and pretty. On the contrary, black was attributed to being bad and ugly.

The last question asked by the researchers was considered the worse since by that point, most of the black children had already identified the black doll as the bad one. Among the subjects, 44% said the white doll looked like them. In past tests however, many of the children refused to pick either doll or just started crying and ran away.

The results were interpreted as good and reliable evidence that black children had internalized racism caused by being discriminated against and stigmatized by segregation. The study shows the stereotyping of black people as bad and white people as nice and more desirable.

Criticisms of the Study

The study has been criticized for being well known only for the reference in the court case as opposed to the intrinsic and experimental value of the work. Many argue that the study lacks theory and control of variables. According to critics, given that an African American couple was the team who conducted the studies, the desirable outcome of wanting to prove African Americans were negatively stereotyped may have caused some partiality or biases, and may have skewed the results.

We traced our hands and wrote future aspirations and personal goals together

Action Item 3

Challenge

Explain why African Centered tasks help students affirmatively answer the question "Who am I?" Considering your students and your community, what kinds of holistic applications might be most engaging and meaningful?

What can a student's self-perception in relation to their race reveal about them academically?

Chapter 4
RESEARCH ON CULTURAL RELEVANCY IN URBAN COMMUNITIES

OBJECTIVES: By the end of this chapter the reader will be able to:

- Discuss and interpret the perceptions of African Centered Curriculums and the impact on schools programs.
- Review and evaluate culturally relevant research.

The field of African Centered Education incorporates culture from countries throughout the continent of Africa and throughout the Diaspora into a rigorous and competitive curriculum. African Centered education includes the use of language, the arts, tradition, ceremony, and values, designed to instill in children a sense of history, responsibility, accountability, community, extended family, propriety, and of course pride. This model has been developed and proven successful over the last forty years by the Institute of Positive Education (Betty Shabazz International Charter School, 1998).

You don't know where you are going unless you know where you came from. Having a rich family history that I knew existed within my own family propelled me forward with a sense of self-confidence. It brought about dignity and intuitive motivation.

Many of our students today don't know their family history and their parents often times don't have the knowledge nor the time to be able to teach family history. Especially single parents working long hours to make ends meet. When are these parents thinking about family history lessons when they are struggling and focused day in and day out on robbing Peter to pay Paul given a poverty mindset. I knew in my elementary school that my great grandmother was the librarian and worked in the school cafeteria where I attended before I was born. The traditions of my family and the school family from generations gave me feelings of pride. I knew my mother was a hard working nurse for twenty-five years. I knew my uncles and cousins who had became professors, doctors, lawyers and war heroes.

RESEARCH ON CULTURAL RELEVANCY

THE IMPORTANCE OF A CULTURAL KNOWLEDGE BASE

Asa G. Hilliard III
SBA
The Reawakening of the African Mind

"Teacher education programs must require some level of proficiency in cultural knowledge about Africans and other people of color. This is especially true if the teacher intends to work with students of color.

It is virtually impossible for teachers to develop a profound respect for their students if they cannot locate students' ancestors in time (chronology) and in space (geography), in terms of the thematic of the evolution of their culture"

I am a direct bi-product of a combination between an urban African-centered and a holistic education. In my research from high school until the present, I have gathered from the following educational theorists that are parallel with my current professional role. I give a brief introduction of the research I found from each theorist on cultural relevant teaching.

Hilliard (1995) argued, if the pursuit of education becomes only content driven in absence of cultural relevancy the authentic evidence of practice becomes meaningless.

Culture therefore organically sustains the human network of relationships that institutionalize the cultural bonds, common interests and social contracts between community practice and cultural reality.

Through the lens of learning rituals, traditions, ceremonies, mores and precepts, culture becomes a critical co-ingredient that supports the purpose and practice of education to life, living and learning.

"RECALL where you come from and therefore who you are, RECLAIM your place in this world, and RENEW yourself, mind, body, and spirit" (Safiyah Institute, 2010).

Bullard (2009) goes further in his argument adding that the traditional practice is to then further project blame and victimization on the students and parents by developing a laundry list of all of their educational defaults, deficits and deficiencies.

The research for the best practices in African Centered Curriculum include creating a classroom culture that fosters cultural relevancy and resiliency in students. Stanton-Salazar & Spina, states that resiliency is a characteristic that enables students to overcome various "at risk" factors including the irrelevancy and demoralizing nature that public schooling has provided

Fardowsa Hajir Director Jones teaches after-school English Language at The Nashville International Center for Empowerment

RESEARCH ON CULTURAL RELEVANCY

Stanton-Salazar & Spina concluded that to build resiliency and success, programs ought to move "away from assimilationist conformity paradigms and toward a rendition of resiliency and success that translates into learning to effectively 'participate in power."

Therefore, resiliency is best facilitated when an individual engages in a process that connects one to a group, identifies available resources, and establishes relationships with key individuals within that group.

Research formulated by the African Centered Education taskforce in Kansas City, Missouri, examined a trend in schools that utilized culturally relevant instructional approaches. These schools often outperformed their counter-parts in similar geographical and demographical areas.

In establishing validity in their research study, the African Centered taskforce found a key ingredient to academic success in urban education. The taskforce began consulting with educational theorist who was grounded in culturally relevant based instructional models like Dr. Jacob Carruthers.

Director Jones teaches Adult English Language at The Nashville International Center for Empowerment

Dr. Jacob Carruthers is the founder and former director of the association for the study of classical African civilizations. In his book Intellectual Warfare, Carruthers (1999) exposes the African influence on past civilizations, as well as present modern day society. He defends the key role ancient African civilizations had and still have on western society. He hopes to improve education practices for generations to come by recognizing the urgency to defend and honor ancient African civilizations.

Similarly, cultural relevant theorist Dr. Asa Hilliard (1997) studied the Re-Awakening of the African mind. Hilliard points out the clearly defined definition of genocide against African people, but goes further to point out the easy to identify and not so easy to identify past and present covert forms of genocide produced by slavery, lynching, legal systems, educational systems, and public health systems.

Dr. Hilliard (1998) in his book African Power: Affirming African Indigenous Socialization in the Face of Culture Wars, articulates the power behind studying, understanding, and practicing African indigenous socialization methods that are important in today's society. Hilliard addresses the attempts and transmissions of the African culture and how the African culture is being suppressed.

The literature asserts that in understanding the importance of the attempts and transmissions of African culture and how it is being suppressed, there is need to look deeper to find the reasons why this has emerged.

Research led me to examine the Isis Papers written by Dr. Francis-Cress Welsing. Welsing (1997) reported a collection of essays. She presents 'The Cress Theory of Color-Confrontation and Racism'. This book gives her psychogenetic theory and global overview of the white supremacy system in America and its impact on black people.

What is the significance of relaying this information to the educators who teach in the urban public school settings? This task is extremely important in order to detect the current issue and correct it.

RESEARCH ON CULTURAL RELEVANCY

Wilson (1992) reported in Awakening the Natural Genius of Black Children, a book for educators who work in an urban setting. The critical reflectional thought that Amos Wilson forces the reader to reflect upon is extremely crucial in understanding their psychosocial values that subconsciously are transmitted to students through teaching. The subconsciously transmitted teaching of educators to black students can be damaging in more than one way. Teachers must explore those damaging ways in which educating can affect academic achievement and the numerous other ways damage can occur to black students if not nurtured correctly.

Likewise, Wortham (1995) stated that "Afro-Centrism is not the answer for Black students in American society." Wortham asserted that education in a multicultural society should practice general concepts, not African culture principles. The idea behind Wortham's notion was thinking African-Centeredness would create separatism and segregation from the education opportunities and the success of students would be jeopardized. Wortham suggest students successes are further dependent upon their integration into American society.

However, Thompson (2004) examined through Ebony Eyes, what teachers need to know but are afraid to ask about African-American students. This book is written for teachers, administrators, and researchers who are impacted by the culturally sensitive issues. This book deals with how teachers view African-American students and how these beliefs and attitudes affect teacher instructional practices and student achievement.

Perry, Steele, & Hilliard III (2003) collectively contributed one essay to the promotion of Young, Gifted and Black students in America. They share common viewpoints and perspectives on the experiences and achievements of African-American students in schools, but evils and wicked problems that face African-American students point to several educational practices that are a direct effect of the underdeveloped students. The scholars argue that with the correction of these educational practices they can promote excellent achievement in African-American students.

RESEARCH ON CULTURAL RELEVANCY

Some of the educational practices that promote excellent achievement in African-American students are presented by Dr. Jawanza Kunjufu. Kunjufu (2000) argues the importance of developing positive self-image and discipline in Black children. Jawanza Kunjufu's objective in writing this book is to expose the character traits in Black children that are not being developed in the school settings of America.

This underdevelopment allows for students to fail not only in academics, but these students will fail in life as well if left untreated and uncorrected. Kunjufu (2008) gives over one-hundred ways to teach Black children, but contends to educators that if they have negative attitudes towards black children or they do not know the children and don't want to learn about the culture and the history of Black children, then the strategies and activities addressed will not be effective inside of the classroom of these educators.

Dr. John Clark (1994) received international recognition for his in depth knowledge from individuals such as Dr. Jacob Carruthers, Dr. Asa Hilliard, Dr. John G. Jackson, Dr. Cheikh Anta Diop, Malcolm X, Dr. Kwame Nkrumah Ghana's first president, Martin Luther King Jr., Richard Wright, Zora Neale Hurston, James Baldwin, Paul Robeson and many more significant others.

Education for a new Reality in the African World was originally prepared for The Phelps-Stokes fund and delivered by Dr. Clark during a ceremony in which he was presented with the highest award offered by the Phelps-Stokes; The Aggrey Medal. John Clark has been recognized for his unique contributions to our knowledge and understandings of ancient African civilization.

This essay is intended to showcase the educational challenge of African people in the 21st century. Clark (1994) argues that despite the hidden truths of African Civilization in Western curricula, Africa's gifts to world societies are rich and essential. Dr. John Henrik Clarke was an avid reader, researcher, professor, master teacher, author, historian and scholar; rich in the cultural experiences of Africa and the people of African descent across the global diaspora.

The Mission Continues 1st Platoon Leader April Jones gets 75 students prepared for back to school with supplies, food and motivation for success in Nashville at the SAC 5K Back 2 School Fundraiser at Fisk University

RESEARCH ON CULTURAL RELEVANCY

In the third edition of Psychology of Blacks: An African Centered Prospective (Ajamu, Adisa; Parham, Thomas A.; White, Joseph L., 1999), researched information about the limitations of traditional psychological theories and approaches when applied to Blacks or African descent people. This source gives a detailed description on the definition of the African Centered viewpoint. The authors of this book goes further into detail in establishing a link between the African American in America to the original traditions, values and spiritual essence of their African ancestors in an attempt to acknowledge the importance of the connection in addressing some of the challenges African descent people will have during the twenty-first century (Ajamu et al., 1999).

Stolen Legacy; written by George G.M. James is a paperback book that has been considered one of the top 100 greatest books of all time. James (2009) addressed the stolen legacy of ancient Africans and considers that Greek philosophy, pre-Socratic, and Athenian philosophers gained their knowledge from the teachings of Egyptians. If the teachings are originally from Egyptians, then it is noteworthy to declare the ancestral rights of the African scholars.

This stolen legacy theory is supported by Khamit Indus Kush and What They Never Told You in History Class, Indus (2000) discusses the stolen legacy of African people referring to historical documents. African civilization was denied their creation of philosophy, science, mathematics, astronomy, architecture, writing, medicine, humanity, and civilization, Christianity, Judaism and Islam. He discusses, prior to the European slave trade, African civilization was celebrated, thrived and was respected as Kings and Queens and innovators.

We find further validation of the stolen legacy when we read Sertima (2003) They Came Before Columbus: The African Presence in Ancient America. Professor Van Sertima was teaching at Rutgers University at the time of publication. He has published numerous poems, critical essays and a Swahili dictionary of legal terms. In this book, the Guyanese historian states his claim through hidden history and research that Africans were introduced to the new world centuries before Columbus arrived in 1492.

RESEARCH ON CULTURAL RELEVANCY

Nobles (1986) calls for the re-awakening of the human spirit in African Psychology: Towards its Reclamation, Reascension and Revitalization. This human spirit is what Dr. Nobles calls "African Psychology", that he argues needs to completely replace the traditional teachings of "White" psychology. Efua (2008) addresses the problem of the achievement gap of African-American students and their White counterparts and includes the correlation between teachers' viewpoint towards culture in the education process and teacher efficacy and how this may affect academic achievement.

Hale-Benson (1986) explores the crucial significance of culture in the education of African-American students. Hale-Benson contends that cultural factors produce group differences that have to be addressed in order for students to excel academically in school.

Ladson-Billings (1994) contends that youth deserve the best from the educator that is responsible for the shaping and molding of their minds. In The Dream Keepers: Successful Teachers of African-American Children, professor of education at the University of Wisconsin, Madison. Ladson-Billings (1994) gives an educational manual that challenges us to look at the deterioration of American public school system and how some educators approach the reincarnation of greatness of quality, value and integrity inside the classroom.

Lewis (2003) asks the question, "could your kids be learning a fourth R at school: reading, writing, 'rithmatic, and race"? In her book Race in the Schoolyard: Negotiating the Color Line in Classrooms and Communities, Lewis (2003) explains how the curriculum, expressed and hidden, conveys many racial lessons. As teachers and administrators deny race inside the school building, it influences the way students view themselves, the world, their community and how they interact with one another.

SAC Spotlight

Madison Mangum is a former student of mine. In second grade Madison was Diagnosed with Oppositional Defiant Disorder (ODD). She would have tantrums in the classroom where all students had to be evacuated. Her parents were always involved and trying to find ways to help Madison academically. Madison is graduating class of 2022 and on track to be the class valedictorian. She graduates from Cora Howe. Cora Howe Exceptional School is a special day school for those students whose learning differences are so significant that they cannot effectively learn within the context of a less restrictive environment. Students are referred through the Individualized Education Plan Team.

Cora Howe specializes in producing standards-based academic programs that are individualized, relevant and differentiated for each child, and we aim to create long-term learning experiences based on areas of interest and strengths for each child. Our students have access to a variety of services and professionals to help achieve academic success, including our library, as well as working-based learning opportunities.

Nurturing their unique students is a dedicated team of caring teachers. Oftentimes, new students will arrive closed off, like the bud of a flower. When they leave, many have totally transformed into something beautiful. Madison's parents said this was the best decision for Madison because other schools had her coloring under a desk in isolation to keep her under control.

RESEARCH ON CULTURAL RELEVANCY

In conclusion, the literature review has revealed that there is a need to identify, address and incorporate African Centeredness methods of reaching African American students, particularly African American students who attend urban public school systems.

Additionally, the literature review suggests that the problems of social integration among African American students are exacerbated by the lack of cultural relevancy experienced by students in American urban public schools. Furthermore, the academic ills and wickedness as pertaining to African American students are a subset and explicitly related to the issues that African Americans encounter amidst the American education system and the historical racist and discriminatory treatment of people of the African descent.

Extending the African Centered curriculum according to research, will improve confidence, self-esteem, motivation and assist with overcoming "at risk" factors thereby directly causing an increase in academic excellence.

Action Item 4

Reflection

How does student progress relate to African Centered Curriculums, the perception and impact on school programs? What are stories from your own life or lives of people close to you that might inspire cultural relevant efficacy in students.

Part III

PERSPECTIVE ON INCLUSION

This is what parental support looks like. Thank you to all of our SAC parents.

AUTHENTIC GUTS

Chapter 5

PHILOSOPHY OF TEACHING: COLLABORATIVE TEACHING IN INCLUSIVE CLASSROOMS

OBJECTIVES: By the end of this chapter the readers will be able to:

- Present goals for students with disabilities
- Discuss the resolution of key challenges
- Identify your own my personal philosophy
- Implement self-reflection strategies as a teaching technique

It is often hard to effectively address students with special needs. Sometimes our children are identified and mislabeled as having a special need or needing special accommodations inside the classroom. Some of those accommodations include students with a need for assistive technology. Assistive technology accommodates children with their disabilities so they can be as successful as their non disabled peers. We can't throw in the towel on our students once they are labeled "special needs" without first taking the necessary assessments and appropriate teaching strategies. Here is an example:

Malcolm gets out of his seat often during class instruction. He fiddles with his pencils until the lead breaks and then he is up at the electric pencil sharpener making all kinds of ruckus. Ms. Locke has repeatedly asked Malcolm to remain in his seat. Malcolm sits back down each time he is instructed to do so, but Ms. Locke has become very frustrated because she can't get through her lesson plan for the day. Ms. Locke spent 3 hours working on her lesson plan last night. Malcolm now needs to throw trash away and has not yet started on the assignment as the rest of the classroom has been doing. Ms. Locke is trying to assist students that have questions, students with side chatter going on when she is distracted by trying to get Malcom to sit back down. Malcolm yells out to Ms. Locke, "can I go to the bathroom please" Ms. Locke ignores him and continues helping another student with the assignment. Malcolm makes the decision to get up and leave the classroom to go to the bathroom. Ms. Locke has had enough, she runs after Malcolm in the hallway and yells at him to get back into the classroom.

After school, Ms. Locke is talking with her teammates in the hallway and says she is going to recommend Malcolm for special accommodations and hopefully she can get him out of her class and placed in the class of all "special needs" students. Some people call this the behavioral classroom, where students unfortunately are reading and writing below grade levels and consistently cause disruptions in the regular education classroom.

PHILOSOPHY OF COLLABORATIVE TEACHING IN INCLUSIVE CLASSROOMS

A Personal Philosophy

GOALS FOR STUDENT LEARNING

Bullard (2009) argued that in the field of urban education, children are routinely damaged as by-products from the professional practice of mis-education, often times in absence of consequence or cause. These children representing the missed educational system are then given the professional labels of being low-performers or under-achievers who didn't study hard enough, were remedial or just not developed enough in their talents to be at grade level.

Often times lack of technology and resources cause setbacks in the operation of the effective classroom management with special need students. Inappropriate and underprepared, we sometimes lack the background knowledge needed to have student success with students with disabilities. Some of our children are visual learners, or audio learners. Some may learn best utilizing "hands on" exploration. What do we do when we have a room full of coworkers, or we are working in a small group together with other individuals who learn differently than we do?

My goals for students with disabilities in the classroom are to ensure they are identified, assessed, evaluated, and equipped with all the necessary tools needed to succeed in school. This includes recognizing their differences and what is needed to respond as an educator to those needs. We don't throw in the towel on Malcolm.

> If I don't know their challenges, learning styles and specific disability (i.e., causes, characteristics and best practices) I can't appropriately and effectively help my students with disabilities reach their goals.

www.thesac.org

GOALS FOR STUDENT LEARNING

My second goal is to effectively communicate with parents of my students, as well as other professionals whom are resourceful in implementing decisions that will benefit my students. If you don't know how to do something, ask! My third goal is to ensure my identified students with disabilities have high self-esteem, self-confidence, and social skills, motivation to succeed and are not rejected, but respected by their peers.

This philosophy comes from my belief that all students can learn and will succeed at attaining their individual goals given culturally appropriate, relevant and practical approaches. This of course is based on their specific needs and individual learning styles.

Some key challenges in the teaching and learning process for students with disabilities in the classroom is time management.
- There is not enough time to identify and assess my students with disabilities.
- I find myself frequently plagued with paperwork and documentation.
- Daily school interruptions that take away from the teaching and learning process.
- Disproportionate teacher-student ratios in the classroom.

STUDENT SUCCESS
BY ANY MEANS NECESSARY

When his 16 year old sister was killed by senseless gun violence on his 14th birthday, we wrapped our arms around him and his family.

AUTHENTIC GUTS

Black Youth Lives Matter

RESOLVING KEY CHALLENGES

After diligently researching, there are several ways to resolve these challenges in the classroom.

One way is by continuing to study the field of special education. In order to become transparent in the meanings, the different disabilities and how best to meet these students needs we must continue to learn.

The second way of meeting challenges of the inclusive classroom is to have effective communication skills. The ability to be respectful, inclusive, inviting and open minded can also resolve these challenges. Most importantly, by involving the families and other professionals, as appropriate, to assist in the thorough education of each student.

The final best solution I see to resolve these challenges is by going above and beyond the job descriptions of an educator to ensure you organize, assess and evaluate appropriately.

This would include lesson planning and often time staying after school a couple hours to prepare instructional materials.

"EDUCATION IS NOT THE FILLING OF A PAIL, BUT THE LIGHTING OF A FIRE."
— W.B. YEATS

#AhNiyahStrong

PHILOSOPHY OF SPECIAL EDUCATION

Tati is an amazing young SAC Scholar

*EDUCATION IS A BETTER SAFEGUARD OF LIBERTY THAN A STANDING ARMY.
– EDWARD EVERETT*

My personal philosophy of special education is that all students learn differently, whether they are special needs or not. If students are presented with culturally relevant and practical approaches they can and will succeed.

Given my personal theory on special education, and using my motivational thinking, my influence on students have always been positive and effective.

I will use that driving force of my personal philosophy to maintain a high standard of performance; remembering my goal in mind, that all students can and will learn.

SAC Scholars

ENACTMENT OF GOALS

NINE-TENTHS OF EDUCATION IS ENCOURAGEMENT – ANATOLE FRANCE

As a member of the Profession of Education and standing on the strength of my personal philosophy on what research says works best,
goals to achieve with special needs students are:

- Problem-Based learning
- Direct Instruction
- Cooperative learning

Another goal for students with disabilities involve teaching them social skills as appropriate.

Ongoing research has suggested that special educators who frequently teach social skills along with ongoing academic instruction have better student outcomes. Through the use of cooperative learning and direct instruction social skills greatly impacts those students.

Problem Based Learning is a useful tool and should be considered a goal for educators. PBL challenges students to learn while learning, encourages students to initiate learning, and strikes their curiosity to learn. This also falls under the lines of cooperative learning.

Kagan strategies and Socratic seminars allow for community circles and the appreciation of other cultures between students. Kagan strategies allow teachers the use of sharing ideas between students and generates student
participation.

Celebrating 10 years of excellence at the 2021 Sankofa Charity Red Carpet Awards Gala

ASSESSMENT OF GOALS

Director Jones leads prayer with her campers before loading up for a summer field-trip

WE CAN PERSUADE OUR CHILDREN POSITIVELY

Before the process of teaching and learning can begin between a teacher and students with disabilities, we first assess their strengths and weaknesses. Make several observations of your students. These observations can be done in the classroom, the lunchroom, and/or the playground etc. In order to know if your students are meeting their goals, a variety of assessments should be used.

The assessments which would guide my instruction was based on the information I attained before planning instruction. I gathered information in the form of formative, summative and performance based assessments (i.e., students demonstrate the knowledge, skills and behaviors along with authentic assessments). One example of assessing goals is by using student portfolios.

By looking through a student's portfolio and using rubrics, an assessment comparison can be made. Goals should've been set in the beginning and placed in the objective section of a student's portfolio. A teacher can better communicate the findings of their students progress and if they are meeting their target goals using this method. This information should be used to instruct further instruction.

Sankofa's Camp Imani at Nashville Wave Country staying active in the summer!

Jaylen Thomas

THEY CANNOT STOP ME. I WILL GET MY EDUCATION, IF IT IS IN THE HOME, SCHOOL, OR ANYPLACE. – MALALA YOUSAFZAI

Within an inclusive classroom, students with a disability must be assessed. General education students will also be assessed, but with differentiation and collaboration. Communication between the team which could include the general education teacher, guidance counselor, parents and special education teachers is one of the most important parts of collaboration. This joint team effort will be able to make recommendations for further student instruction.

Having open dialogues is a popular research based study that I used inside the classroom thereby creating an inclusive learning environment. I believe that educators should have a cultural connection with the students they serve in order to be effective. I believe that every student has a unique history and importance from their family backgrounds that they bring to the classroom if allowed. Promote students to be their own individual and celebrate all of their ideas and thoughts. This is where the magic happens in the classroom.

Everyone can learn something by having cooperative learning experiences embedded in their curriculum. It doesn't matter about the students' socio-economic statuses, every student has a voice. Although differentiation of instruction is necessary to meet the diverse learning styles in the classroom via visual, audio, or hands on, celebration of all students is a must.

Sankofa boys watering their raised garden beds

AUTHENTIC GUTS

REFLECTION ON TEACHING

Wendy was sitting in my 7th grade ELA class. I had each student keep a running record of the bell ringers every morning. The bell ringer is the activity that awaits my students upon entering my room. It's the first thing they see on the board. Usually, I posed a a though provoking question and the students had to respond in their journals. I would collect the journals daily and respond to them with annotations, comments and suggestions. This is meant to be a quick 5-10 minute writing activity. Wendy, would write about dark gloomy nights away from home. She wrote about her girlfriend that she felt she was totally in love with. Wendy sometimes as I recall discussed running away to live happily ever after with her girlfriend. She wrote about no one caring about her as she was a foster child. Academically, Wendy was very intelligent, but because her focus was outside the school building it was hard to see her talent and skills. With low reading scores on assignments, not completing homework assignments she was referred for special education evaluation. Had I not been communicating with Wendy through journaling, I wouldn't have been able to number one, understand and have compassion for her. Two, I would not have known that she has had trauma in her life and needed support. Three, I pulled from my school resources of counselors and team mates to put Wendy in a girls mentorship program after school. Wendy, is now thriving in her high school, she was not misplaced into the special education program and she looks forward to attending cosmetology school upon high school graduation.

Community Fall Festival

AUTHENTIC GUTS

REFLECTION ON TEACHING CONT.

I really believe a mind is a terrible thing to waste. This belief drives my passion as an educator. I use positive reinforcement, constructive criticism and teacher feedback for my students and I think that makes me a stronger teacher.

With continuous personal growth in time management and organization, I realized that my philosophy compared to the philosophy of Heward. He believes all students can learn given the appropriate foundations. The most important building block of that foundation begins with us, the educator being able to identify, assess and evaluate student data.

Becoming an effective teacher in inclusive collaborative teaching includes grasping the appropriate foundation. Meeting all the needs of students is a hard task, but with appropriate planning, and assessment of all students in the inclusion classroom, they can and will succeed.

Just as (Heward, 2013) addresses his belief that not only is the field of special education interesting and informative, it includes the student, parents and families of exceptional children and of teachers and other professionals who work with them to achieve success stories. I too believe "it takes a village to raise a child."

Action Item 5

Challenge

Identify how you will use what you have learned moving forward. How will you present goals for students with disabilities? How will you resolve key challenges of differentiated instruction? How can you use self-reflection as a teaching technique?

Part IV
RESEARCH-BASED STRATEGIES FOR ENGAGING EXTERNAL PARTNERS FOR STUDENT SUCCESS

This is what community support looks like. Thank you to all of our SAC supporters.

Chapter 6
COMMUNITY PARTNERSHIPS IN RURAL COMMUNITIES

> OBJECTIVES: By the end of this chapter the reader will be able to:
>
> - Discuss marked discrepancies between the educational outcomes of urban and rural students
> - Describe ways principals connect with external partners for student success
> - Interpret the development of culturally responsive best practice training processes
> - Summarize the emergent themes and findings of the research

According to incarceration versus education statistics in the United States Of America, $75 billion is spent each year on corrections funding. One hundred thousand dollars is spent per prisoner whereas $10,000 is spent per student each year. There has been over 20 prisons built in the state of California since 1980 and only one university built. As leaders in the field of education these numbers should be alarming. One of the most important but often under researched obligation of the school principal is family and community partnerships. One of the main reasons this is an important obligation of leadership is that there is a strong need for more family and community involvement in schools. In other words, schools can no longer operate in isolation to facilitate the well-being of students if we intend to change our global college population from #65 in the world and #1 highest prison population globally.

Schools, families, and communities must work together to ensure the success of students. Thus, the principal's pursuit of these external partnerships is critical for the success of students, especially students from rural communities.

"Family and friends gathered Monday to memorialize a young Nashville musician who was shot to death outside his home last week. Five youths ages 12 to 16 have been charged with criminal homicide in the death of 24-year-old Kyle Yorlets. Two teens accused in a musicians murder have been formally indicted by a grand jury. Diamond Lewis and Decorrius Wright are each charged with first-degree murder in connection with Kyle Yorlets' death. The Nashville Musician was shot and killed at his West Nashville home in 2019. Roniyah McKnight, 14; Diamond Lewis, 15, and Decorrius Wright, 16, as well as a 12-year-old girl and a 13-year-old boy are all charged in connection with Kyle Yorlets death. Police say Yorlets was killed when the five charged took his wallet and shot him for refusing to give them his car keys, according to police". Nashville, Tenn. (WKRN)

Diamond Lewis was a 2nd grade student of mine. How did *we* as a community let this happen to them? How can *we* as a community prevent our youth from the school to prison pipeline?"

COMMUNITY PARTNERSHIPS

One of the most significant factors to a school's success is the leadership of the principal. Once defined as the primary manager of schools, today's principals have entirely different roles and duties. For example, much research purports that some of the main roles of today's principals include but are not limited to:

- Culture builder
- Resource provider
- Schedule setter
- Program developer
- Policy reviewer

Equally significant is the principal's role in the academic effectiveness of schools. Due to accountability measures, the responsibility of school success has been placed squarely on the principal's shoulders.

That is, principals must be visionaries who inspire and motivate schoolwide commitment to student achievement. In addition, they must excel in providing teachers with instructional leadership.

There is a marked discrepancy between the educational outcomes of urban and rural students. Although not always the case, urban students tend to outperform rural students.

Wise (2010) denoted that one in every four rural high school students dropped out of school. The high school dropout rate in rural areas is 11.1%, while the urban rate is 12.8%. Poverty and geographic isolation limit rural students' access to important community resources. In addition, it has been difficult to achieve quality relationships between homes and schools in rural school settings. According to Semke and Sheridan (2012), some of the main reasons for this disconnect are as follows:

- Lack of identification of the needs of rural families.
- Scheduling conflicts between schools and rural families.
- Limited parental access to transportation to participate in school events.
- Little to no school offerings of nonacademic services that meet the needs of rural families.

COMMUNITY PARTNERSHIPS

61% of rural parents believe public education is failing their children.

An equally significant factor is rural parents' negative stigmatization of the public school system. For example, 61% of rural parents believe public education is failing their children. Although rural parents believe in the potential of schools and teachers, a deeper look revealed that they have less confidence that their schools actually deliver on that promise.

These parents also interact with teachers less frequently relative to urban and suburban schools. Finally, only 54% of rural parents are satisfied with their interactions with school staff members. Because of these conditions, there is a need for rural school principals to connect schools with families and surrounding communities. The principals' pursuit of school-community partnerships is critical for the success of rural students.

In the era of accountability, student achievement is the benchmark used to assess school (California Department of Education, 2010b). With higher student achievement citizens become better educated and produce higher wages, which is helpful for the economy (U.S. Department of Labor). Lastly, both school and community organizations benefit from the financial impact of partnerships by increasing revenue streams to the local school.

I conducted research in order to find ways Principals connect with external partners in order to attain student success in rural communities. The process of data analysis began with me transcribing each Zoom interview into the audio software program Audacity, which were then read and analyzed over several readings. During the first review of Zoom interview transcriptions, themes began to emerge.

Data management processes discern the ways in which themes or concepts were labeled, sorted, and compared (Ritchie et al., 2003). Emergent themes in qualitative social science research are a basic building block of inductive approaches and are derived from real-world research participants through the coding process (Given, 2008).

EMERGENT THEMES

TRUST

INTERGRITY & TRANSPARENCY

TRADITION

COMMUNITY PARTNERSHIPS

The emergent themes are (a) trust, (b) integrity and transparency, and (c) tradition.

This section explains each of the themes that came out during my research. The themes are organized in chronological order of the research questions.

Research questions:
- What are the key leadership practices that influence parent and community partnerships in successful rural elementary schools?

The first and second theme align directly with research question one in that they identify leadership practices and perceptions of rural school principals such as building trust and establishing credibility through integrity and transparency, thereby creating family and community partnerships.

These parents also interact with teachers less frequently relative to urban and suburban schools. Finally, only 54% of rural parents are satisfied with their interactions with school staff members. Because of these conditions, there is a need for rural school principals to connect schools with families and surrounding communities. The principals' pursuit of school-community partnerships is critical for the success of rural students.

54% of rural parents are satisfied with their interactions with school staff members.

The third theme, tradition, aligns with the second, third, and final research question in that it identifies how (a) families and community partnerships contribute to school success, and (b) ways in which families partner and contribute to student and school success. Many of the interview participants spoke about rich traditions and multigenerational families who are vested in the school and community.

In addition to rich community history, Principal 3 expressed that she was born, raised, and will die right in the district she works. Many of the teachers and staff members have taught one another or their parents and continue to raise their families together in their small rural community.

Theme 1: Trust

This particular theme played a major role in the research process. Trust, and its necessity, emerged throughout all the Zoom interviews. Each principal referenced the establishment of trust. Leithwood and Riehl (2003) also denoted that educational culture of families is strengthened when school leaders promote trust and communicate with teachers and families. When asked how trust has been cultivated between parents and the community, Principal 1 responded that building trust comes with building your own integrity and character.

Principal 1 further explained that parents understand making mistakes, and as long as you admit to your mistakes, you gain their trust. If you are always honest, even when it hurts, the parents understand that you are working with them to do what is right for their child.

I try to explain to every parent I meet that we all do the best we can with the information that we have at that moment in time. Parents do the same things. As long as they know my decisions are made out of careful thought, even if they disagree with me, they know I think I am doing what is best for everyone involved. The same things hold true for our community members. We have to respect each other even if we do not understand or agree all the time.

Due to COVID-19, it has been a challenge to cultivate a welcoming environment.

Principal 2 stated this relationship strengthens over time. It's not an overnight feat; rather, it's a repeated success. The principal went on to explain:

Parents count on me and trust me to make the decisions that are in the best interest of their children's education. Building a partnership with the parents and community is how we attain that relationship. Trust has to come before anything.

Principal 2 continued explaining that in the past years, the school has tried to have people present for the students from the community. Parent nights, involvement nights, and reaching out to caregivers to ensure they have what they need to help promote their children's education have been integral to doing so.

Principal 3 believes to build trust with parents and community, you have to be open and available. She further explained that the trust factor is built when you listen to the needs of the families because they just want to be heard. Being upfront and trusting the education process were other ways she builds trust with parents and the community.

Theme 1: Trust

Principal 4 fought to gain trust from the parents. Being a new school with parents being accustomed to the primary school's way of doing things, it was a challenge to have all unfamiliar teachers along with a new school building in a recently created district.

In order to build trust, the teachers of this school were required by the principal to introduce themselves and establish a communication link with all the parents. With time, trust was no longer an issue or focus for the families because they trust the school and principal to do what they are supposed to do in the best needs of their children.

Principal 5 worked to establish positive parental communication in the beginning of the year. Monthly family nights that engaged parents and the community with activities were a way trust was established at her school. She believes parents will feel better appreciation during the school year when positive communication is established before the potential need for negative communications occur.

Principal 4 cultivates a welcoming school environment for parents, businesses, and community leaders because she is in her natural element. She shares that she was born, raised, and will die in the house she lives in, which is right next to her mother's residence. In fact, Principal 4 attended the elementary school within the community. Subsequently, she feels very comfortable and relatable to the parents and people in her community.

Southern Word can be found at www.southernword.org

As a school community partner, I partnered with other community organizations to expose my SAC Scholars to various forms of performing arts, all the humanities, academic support, cultural experiences, etc.

Southern Word sent in a trained teacher, worked closely with each student, using writing prompts and encouragement to go deeper, tighter, more rhythmically to create a spoken word poem or speech. They then worked with them on delivery, working on stage presence, articulation, emphasis and rhythm. The workshops I've had them do for me in the past lasted 4 weeks, twice a week, and culminated in a poetry slam (competition) with other workshop students from other schools, and can result in the student moving on to the next level of competition.

It is a very urban art form, most likely to be about the African American experience, but not always, and exactly what these kids need--the opportunity to express themselves in a safe, accepting environment.

Pat Blankenship - The CATT
The Children's Academy Theatre of Tennessee

Principal 5 believes cultivating a welcoming school environment for parents starts with the teachers and the staff in the building. The building culture collectively builds strong relationships with parents and families. Due to the COVID-19 pandemic, the relationships have grown stronger than ever, which has made a notable difference in student achievement.

By modeling expected and ethical behavior, the principal communicates the important values and principles of the school (Reed & Kensler, 2010; Reeves, 2008). Parent-professional partnerships can result in a variety of benefits for students when the two rely and depend on one another and engage in shared-decision making (Haines et al., 2013).

These benefits include enhanced academic gains, increased behavioral achievement, and improved attendance rates (Bryan & Henry, 2012). Principal 1 makes herself available in her small community. The approach to involving families, businesses, and community leaders in the decision-making process of her school with parents begins when students are in kindergarten. Additionally, the elders in the community church assist. Further, the building is always clean, and parents are consistently involved in making decisions.

Principal 2 has a leadership team, which includes at least one parent. There are parent advisory committees established as part of a district initiative that includes parental participation. At least one parent is on the school's tier 1 team, which includes the behavior plan of the school and how it functions. Parents bring a different perspective and fresh ideas to the school. When they have questions, this is the opportunity where they can get addressed.

COMMUNITY PARTNERSHIPS
Theme 1: Trust

When Principal 3 was asked to describe her approaches to involving families, businesses, and community leaders in the decision-making processes of the school, she acknowledged employing several approaches. The first of which is having meetings, teacher conferences, Parent Teacher Association (PTA) and Parent Teacher Organization (PTO) meetings for Title I decisions. They have parent engagement, and committees have a voice in how to spend expenditures. As a result, the community takes ownership because they have a vote.

These collaborations have impacted student's success because they share knowledge with the families and community. The decisions made that include parent's votes allow the parent to see the successes of their children firsthand. For example, the community together selected a reading program called IReady. The parents are shown the end results of the progress their child has made, and this strengthens the collaborations.

Principal 4 overall is pleased and believes her school does a good job with involving parents in decision-making processes. She acknowledges there is room to grow in the area of reaching out to business and community leaders. The school has a family engagement committee that meets every 2 to 3 months where the parents give school staff feedback, and in turn, the staff educates parents on the school's test scores and other relevant data. Principal 5 outreaches verbally and has those conversations in the community and with families face to face. She does so because "that works best for us."

Principal 1 explained that collaboration with families, business owners, and community leaders has been challenging because of the pandemic, and she explained how communication typically occurs. Our families know they can contact me at any time via email, text, or phone calls. We have very few businesses in our rural community. Many times, the collaboration comes from our central office staff who are members of the Chamber of Commerce or other memberships. One way our district communicates and collaborates with business leaders is they provide a districtwide newsletter to the chamber each month. In non-pandemic years, family members are invited into the school at least once per month for an activity or a school-wide program. This also gives them access to the school staff.

There are very few businesses in this community. One of the challenges for rural schools is the lack of business. Principal 1 explained that "our school is in the middle of family farms. One of our businesses happens to be the bus contractors." The leadership team makes most of the decisions. Many of the staff members live in the community and our local staff members represent the people in the community. We have PTO officers that meet monthly to discuss decisions and to give input to the decision-making process.

COMMUNITY PARTNERSHIPS

The families and the community members understand there are high expectations for their students. "They also understand we will push our students to do their best. I believe, because of the positive culture in the building, parents know we are doing our best as well," explained Principal 1. The positive publicity the school has received in the past coupled with the school level of effectiveness scores has established that the "community is aware we want to be the best in the state." When it comes to needing their support with attendance, homework, and so on, families and community members alike are willing to give us what we need.

Principal 2 responded that they work to ensure that parents and families have the necessary tools and support systems in place to assist each child with his or her learning. She continued explaining how those from the area contribute to the school's success. We have partnerships with businesses in the community who not only provide financial support, but human capital. They send employees over to the school to assist with different activities for our students. Many of our teachers are out in the community and being a part of the community. Although it does not show up on a report card, it helps when parents and students see their teachers placed in the community doing other things than just teaching.

7th Grade ELA was my favorite teaching experience, but it also was so physically draining that I was neglecting my own son. I was coaching the varsity girls basketball team, teaching 7th graders and by the time I got home there was no quality time for my middle school son who was home alone after school. I cried and cried when I sent my son back to Chicago to live with his father. I felt like a shit bag of a mother. I was sending my son away because I couldn't help him meanwhile I got up everyday to help hundreds of other parents children.

Stratford High School Nashville, TN

Principal 3 has family engagement nights where snacks are provided, and the atmosphere is relaxed as they teach their parents how to work with their children. Due to the current pandemic, the teachers have been using Zoom and Google meets with parents to provide engagement strategies for their students. This is because many parents and caregivers do not know how to effectively use technology during a time when the school has been forced to hold classes virtually.

Principal 4 has a Title 1 committee and a parent engagement committee. These committees meet, which allows for collaboration to take place between parents and school leadership. The principal explains that "this gives the opportunity to communicate wonderfully with parents." She encourages and employs different strategies in order to effectively collaborate with business and community leaders.

Principal 5 collaborates with families during family nights, sending student agendas home, and providing communication notebooks on a daily basis. In addition, texts are sent to parents and guardians through the Remind application. Parent teacher conferences and school-wide callouts are other ways in which collaboration takes place at this school.

AUTHENTIC GUTS

COMMUNITY PARTNERSHIPS

Principal 3 comments that she is transparent when delivering information about school dynamics to the community. For example, a communication newsletter highlighting what the school is doing goes out to parents and the community. In addition, the marquee outside the building is updated with appreciation of teachers because she wants the community to know and appreciate their school and staff. Another communication tool is social media, which Principal 3 says is used to share the dynamics of the school with anyone who follows.

Principal 4 has meetings at the beginning of the school year, which allow parents and the other community members to walk through the school where information booths are set up. This is done as she believes parents and community stakeholders must have a clear and definitive understanding of school dynamics in order to build a productive relationship with all parties involved. Activities such as hosting back-to-school bashes, sharing through social media pages, and using the local community newspaper all help provide clear direction of the school and how it operates.

Director Jones sits in her office at the former SAC Headquarters located 1817 Jefferson Street

Theme 2: Integrity and Transparency

Principal 5 addresses the commissioner and invites them to tour the building. She comments that providing transparency of the building operations is important. The principal and staff reach out to parents and school board members as an approach to developing the community's understanding of expectations, safety procedures, and other policies. Parents and community members are able to find information on social media and Facebook pages in order to foster communication. Further, phone calls are made from school staff, and agenda books are sent home regularly to parents.

During the Zoom interview process, multiple questions were asked about family and community partnership and how they can contribute to a school success. The responses varied in terms of the dynamics of the individual school communities and whether or not businesses and resources were available. According to Principal 1, a way that she approaches addressing the community's understanding of school dynamics is through clearly describing the expectations. Being a small community, Principal 1 discussed the importance of her building personal character: "Following through on your words and actions, and being available for parents, makes a huge difference in student success."

COMMUNITY PARTNERSHIPS

Principal 2 developed his community's understanding of school dynamics through promoting and sharing the operations, strategies, and expectations the school fosters, which is especially important for parents. He further said, "We make sure to be honest and open on how and where to find help when needed for our community. This year due to the pandemic, the integrity and communication is higher than ever before." He continued saying he had to "support our families during the pandemic out of necessity. Teachers had to reach out more, and partnerships were strengthened because of the clear and direct communication approaches."

When asked about what has been done to position the school as a "community school," Principal 1 stated, "I have not made the school a community school; it was that way when I came, and all I have to do is keep up the tradition of taking care of their children." She goes further and describes the school's rich history and it being at the heart of their community before she arrived. A few staff members have also had their parents, siblings, and extended family attend the school. The rich tradition of being a "community school" is further fostered through the long-tenured teachers, and some have been working there for over 25 years.

Principal 2 discussed the partnership between the elementary school and the only high school in the county. He commented on the relatively unique situation and its role in cultivating tradition with community members: Schools share the same campus, and we have built a partnership with them.

We allow our school to be used by the community as much as possible. With our school having all of the disabled students in the community, we have hosted a fundraising pageant for the students with disabilities. We build trust by being available for our community and allow them to be involved.

Principal 3 described the school where she was employed for many years as the pillar of the community before the pandemic. She recalled that "the school is the community." For example, she described about having the traditional Fall Festival, selling school t-shirts, and involving the entire community in its events and programs brought everyone together. The community has multigenerational families who have lived there and attended the school. The parents traditionally walked the halls of the schools, the community held car shows at the school, and people would come and generally talk about the rich tradition of the school. It has been extremely hard for the community with the realization that it is soon closing.

COMMUNITY PARTNERSHIPS
Theme 3: Tradition

Principal 4 has a 50% poverty rate and provides many resources to families in the community in order to foster a feeling of tradition. The community church assists with providing help for families through the school, which includes providing meals for students and families in need.

The "Farms to Families" program helps to feed the community, and the principal personally delivers many, if not all, of these food boxes. There are not many local businesses nearby to engage with the school. Further, parents also do not have many opportunities to visit and engage with students. Principal 4 shared that students "are at a stage where they, quite frankly, don't want their parents at school with them very often. Sometimes some parents will eat lunch with their child."

Principal 5 opens the school building up to the community and consistently invites and ask for parental involvement and volunteers to assist with school functions. The school and its staff conduct service projects in the community and give back to the community. Principal 5 shared that she tries "to make our school the focal point of the community."

When the question was asked how would the principal assess his or her effectiveness in connecting families to resources that are outside of the school, Principal 1 responded that she has very limited community resources. She said that "the best we can do is first and foremost find the needs of our families, and then we search for the resources." She continued by saying that the "county has a Student Services Director, and she is usually our first point of contact for family needs." Principal 1 further shared the "first option is to see if the staff or the area churches can help. If it is bigger than we can handle, we turn to the central office staff for support." Principal 1 recalled that in her 14 years as part of the school community, "there have been few times we have not found a solution to most family problems."

Principal 2 believes he has done a good job connecting families to resources that are outside of the school; however, there have been needs that have arisen that were not present before the pandemic.

He said, "We had to go virtual, so we needed our families without internet to be taken into consideration. We also have families who have needs that we don't know about. This goes back to the trust factor. When parents trust us, they can call on us for needs and support."

COMMUNITY PARTNERSHIPS

Principal 3 assessed her effectiveness in connecting families to resources outside of the school in a positive way. The district has a family resource center, which assists families with food, power bills, and clothing. Her students are exposed to the community outside of their own via field trips.

They also have a summer feeding program provided to them through the 21st Century grant. Similarly, Principal 4 assessed her effectiveness as very effective. The parents know they can call upon her and seek assistance when in need of help or assistance.

Principal 5 feels she is very effective based on the tremendous amount of community support. For example, the partnerships established between the school and juvenile courts, Department of Child Services (DCS) have manifested into a trusting and growing relationship. She shared, "The community and parents call on us, and we call on them." Her self-effectiveness is rated 9 out of 10 on a success scale for connecting families to resources that are outside of the school.

With relatively little research focused on the unique needs and difficulties of rural areas, rural impoverished youth have been described as the forgotten children (Farmer & Hamm, 2015). Many economically-disadvantaged youths attend underprivileged school districts.

These rural districts experience a variety of challenges that adversely impact academic achievement (Farmer & Hamm, 2016). A number of studies show that the rural principal must dedicate time and effort toward forming strong school-community relations (Educating Students in Rural America, 2016).

Sankofa's Camp Imani at Tennessee State University gardening with the Carrie Mae Williams Center. The Carrie Mae Williams Center is a nonprofit education and intervention organization dedicated to cultivating the minds, bodies, and spirits of youth and young adults.
www.carriemaewilliamscenter.org

COMMUNITY PARTNERSHIPS

*This section concerns the question-
What are the key leadership practices that influence parent and community partnerships in successful rural elementary schools?*

Through analysis of principal Zoom interviews, it was identified that building trust and establishing credibility through integrity and transparency influences successful parent and community partnerships in successful rural elementary schools. Most of the principals believed that establishing trust and delivering on promises are overall the most meaningful actions that can be done to create school community partnerships.

During the Zoom interview process, principals were asked the question: "What are the most important things they do to create school community partnerships?" Principal 1 discussed the importance of being open and transparent with families and caregivers: Always let the parent know that we are all collectively doing what's right for their children and them and own up to your mistakes. Never be afraid to apologize as a leader when a mistake is made. Being transparent is how credibility is established between parents and community stakeholders.

From this response, we can deduce that honesty is an important component in building successful relationships in rural communities. Principal 2 agreed when he also pointed out the importance of setting and maintaining high expectations for oneself: "If you don't have a trust factor, a lot of the other things doesn't really matter." Principal 3 responded that you have to physically reach out to the community "the old fashion way" in order to build trusting relationships with businesses. With the responses of these three principals, it appears that trust is ultimately the most relevant leadership practice rural principals do in achieving student success.

Other strategies are also utilized by principals in order to help build rapport with the community and families. Principal 4 shared that the love that she has for her students spreads to their homes where parents and grandparents know that she cares for her students. They ultimately trust that she will make the best decisions for their children. Principal 4 shared that "it is important that they know us; we have to be visible - waving at parents in the morning and saying good evening after school."

Howard Gentry pictured here with Dr. Jones, serves the Metropolitan Government of Nashville as the Criminal Court Clerk of Davidson County in the Twentieth Judicial District. A Nashville native, Gentry was elected three times to countywide public office. He was a Metro Council member-at-large before being elected Metro Nashville-Davidson County's first African American vice mayor. He was re-elected in 2003. In 2007, Gentry was a candidate for Mayor and narrowly missed the run-off by less than 300 votes. He received his B.S. and master's degrees in education from Tennessee State University.

Principal 5 responded that building relationships with children and families is overall the most important thing that can be done to create school community partnerships. Principal 5 said, "I want parents to know that I am here to help kids be the best that they can be. Kids will do things for you when they know you care." She continued by saying family and communities will follow suit when high expectations are set for the community and families.

COMMUNITY PARTNERSHIPS

This section concerns these questions:

1. What family and community partnership can contribute to a school's success?

2. What can families practice or do to partner with the school to ensure student success?

3. How can the community contribute to the school's success?

During Zoom interviews, the principals gave varying responses when asked how each would define school-community partnerships. For example, Principal 1 believes building one's own character as a leader in the community, hiring good people, and making connections with parents at the beginning of the school year creates a solid foundation for school-community partnerships.

Principal 1 shared a few of the ways in which this foundation is established at her school. It is a tradition to have a community ice cream social meet and greet with parents and community stakeholders. Another example is that during field day, parents and community members are greeted at the door and welcomed in. These events are happily anticipated by the community annually. The connections that are made during kindergarten are continued through high school in this small rural community.

Principal 2 discusses the community being very involved due to multigenerational families. He feels that it is a good situation when parents and grandparents are meaningfully involved.

Nashville-Davidson County's Juvenile Court Judge Sheila Calloway, the Juvenile Court Magistrates, and the employees of Juvenile Court are responsible for making sure every child and parent who passes through their court is met with justice, fairness, and hope. As described by Tennessee Code Annotated Section 37-1-101, the purpose of juvenile court is: "To provide for the care, protection, and wholesome moral, mental and physical development of the children coming within its provisions." Using evidence based programs and services, Nashville's Juvenile Court and the youth and families it serves are LEADING THE WAY.

Yet, Principal 2 also recalled, "It was a challenge in the beginning for me because my previous school consisted of 230 students as opposed to now being in a city type setting school with 600 students in a very rural setting."

Principal 3 has had many successes with community and parent inclusion. For example, a tradition in her community now, after receiving a 21st Century grant for the past 17 years, has allowed the community to be a part of the process in receiving and decision making for expenditures of this grant. As part of the grant, the school reaches out to the district's nutrition department to provide students with healthy after-school snacks. The community also knows they can expect to receive boxes of food, clothing, and even Christmas gifts due to the established partnership.

Principal 4 is now at a new school that was created as an intermediate school. The school is a combination of four 5th grade and 6th grade classes from the middle school. These students matriculated from a K-4 school where they and their parents were "babied." This compounded with the school being new created a challenge for teachers in the beginning. Trust had to be built first, but with time and teachers building relationships with parents, a strong school community was created. Principal 4 shared that this was done through making the school, its staff, and students visible by having the administration and teachers introduce themselves in the beginning of the school year, by having students support local nursing homes by sending sympathy cards, and by having the school community complete several food drives for the local food shelter. These are ways in which Principal 4 has developed school community partnerships.

COMMUNITY PARTNERSHIPS

On November 4, 2014, Bill Haslam was re-elected Tennessee's governor with the largest victory in modern Tennessee history.
Under his leadership, Tennessee was recognized as a national leader in education, economic development, efficient and effective government and fiscal strength.
Since 2011, Tennessee students have been the fastest improving in the country in academic achievement. High school graduation rates are at an all-time high, and Tennessee is the first state in the nation to offer high school graduates and adults two years of community or technical college free of tuition and mandatory fees.

Principal 5 worked especially hard to establish a good relationship with parents before COVID-19 arrived. It took 3 years to build this solid foundation for parents, which was bolstered through reaching out to churches for assistance.

Principal 5 shared, "Our students have grown in state test scores, and it's because we continually are reaching out and getting family involvement with our parents." The high expectations these school leaders set ensure parents and the community have a strong relationship built through tradition, trust, and transparency. This allows for a two-way access between school and community.

Using Hitt and Tucker's (2016) framework which identifies five domains that describes effective school leadership practices.

The domains describe broad areas of leadership while the dimensions describe specific leadership practices. The domains are as follows with following examples:

- Establishing and conveying the vision: Meeting and inviting parents, community members and stakeholders with welcoming arms and verbal expectations for the school's vision and mission for students.
- Building professional capacity: Allowing teachers to have professional development opportunities regularly in the area of concern and needs of the students.
- Creating a supportive organization for learning: Enhancing diversity through instructional content. Building a supportive climate for diverse learning in the school and the community.
- Facilitating a high-quality learning experience for students: All students feel respected and included inside the classroom and within the community.
- Connecting with external partners: Reaching out to the community "the old fashion way" knocking on doors with a smile.

Through conducting this study, it was found that rural school principals overall have a way of establishing partnerships that are conducive to their small rural communities. Although all these schools are in rural communities, the dynamics differ between each one. Yet similarly, the principals took full responsibility for their successful leadership practices in building family and community partnerships for student success. They all have a passion and love for their schools and the work they do in their communities. They feel equipped to deal with situations that require community and family engagements within their schools.

Some principals have more resources within their communities than other rural communities, but all the principals assessed their effectiveness with getting the resources they need for their students as highly effective. In other words, they are very satisfied with the results received within their families and communities.

Some principals, however, confirmed they lack in the area of reaching out for funding. Principal 4 shared, "We don't have sports at my school, so I don't do a lot with reaching out for funding." This is missed opportunities to expand outreach for students. Oversight in acquiring additional funding opportunities happens to be one of the key challenges rural school principals face (Farmer & Hamm, 2016).

COMMUNITY PARTNERSHIPS

Through conducting this study, it has been determined that further rural elementary school principals can be mentored in fostering and maintaining community relationships to help provide necessary resources and tools for students and their families in these rural communities. A type of 'train the trainer' program used as part of a collaborative community process could prove beneficial for school principals, parents, and stakeholders invested in the success of students.

The development of a culturally responsive best practice training processes, that specifically addresses the challenges facing rural schools, is crucial. This process is beneficial for multi-generational families, community members, and for potential new area residents that seek to go into an unfamiliar world of small rural communities, as it helps them to understand more specifically how places such as these operate.

The training process could allow administrators the opportunity to focus and design a school community environment that is conducive for student success and is driven by intimate school community partnerships.

Ultimately being able to handle situations that arise and then ensure that students and families are both safe and comfortable within the school community is the duty of the principal. Principals who do not readily have training in school collaborative processes could benefit in community partnerships trainings that assist with 'finding a way when there is no way.' School principals need the knowledge and capabilities that requires them to go out into the community to attain, establish, and maintain necessary resources and tools for students.

The overall benefactor from this study is that school and community partnerships are beneficial for student success in rural schools. This form of relationship must flow between all parties involved: parents, businesses, and community leaders. Each of these groups should feel that they have clarity in understanding the dynamics of how their school community works.

When there are not many businesses and resources to pull from, the manner in which parents, business leaders, and principals are specifically trained on how to effectively work together is vital. A community coalition that trains the leaders and community stakeholders could potentially benefit students in rural areas to exceed academic and social expectations even further and continue to close the academic disparities gap between urban and rural students.

Dr. Jones leads the way during the Annual Sankofa Charity Ride with support from motorcyclist across the nation as they merge to ride for youth and education.

Action Item 6

Challenge

Develop a culturally responsive community event. Connect with schools, families, and external partners. How can you use the themes and findings of the research to help overcome marked discrepancies between the educational outcomes of urban and rural students?

Part V

FUTURE DIRECTION

Chapter 7

CLOSING COMMENTS

I have been in some very scary positions in my short life. I don't disregard and try to forget those experiences of my past. I use all of that knowledge and draw from it when I need to reach a student who needs support. It brings a different teaching method and approach when we build a rapport with the student. Students will trust you if you show that you care and sometimes the only way to show you care to a student is by being relatable. I am human and we have all experienced trials and tribulations.

CLOSING COMMENTS

With over 15 years of teaching experience from the west side and the south side of Chicago to the north and east side of Nashville's urban environments, I decided to take my own tip and follow another pathway. I'm well emerged in urban settings, but what about the forgotten students in rural America? Can I bring my theories and best practices to an unfamiliar territory and master student success? I wonder if I can get involved in the community and make a difference in an area where everyone knows everyone and I will be looked upon as an outsider by the community.

Now having established my life in the rural community of Tipton County, I have already began engaging my community. I would like to utilize all of my past experiences to help students and adults reach their full attention in the district. I was just hired as the Site Director of the School Age Child Care program at Brighton Elementary School. I have been also hired to teach adult education in my county, provide services to adults to build the knowledge and skills necessary for high school equivalency (HiSET), employment, post-secondary opportunities, and economic self-sustainability. "It's never too late to get an education,"

The School Age Child Care program provides before and after school child care to school-aged children enrolled in Tipton County Schools. Additionally, the SACC offers full-day care when school is not in session such as in-service training days, holidays, and summer.

SACC focuses on child-centered activities and developmentally appropriate practices. Our program strikes a healthy balance between free-choice and teacher-directed activities; stimulating and quiet activities; large and small group activities. Typically rotations at many of our SACC Sites include hands-on learning experiences, games, physical activity, homework help, reading and/or math tutoring, arts and crafts, and computer time. I look forward to designing my own culturally relevant curriculums for education seekers. I'm hoping to get into some "good trouble" in continuing to positively impact our youth. I'm in the preventive business of catching the youth early before challenges arise, but when challenges do arise they have been instilled and understand the key to overcoming life ups and downs is knowledge of self. As an education leader, continue ensuring after trials and tribulations for us adults who have had challenges in their lives have the opportunity to continue learning. Stay tuned as I further continue bringing sustainability and community care for our youth as well as the community-at-large.

Thank you for reading Authentic Guts!

Dr. April A. Jones
EXECUTIVE
DIRECTOR
WWW.THESAC.ORG

Dr. April "Remy" Jones as some know me are well acquainted with my enjoyment for riding motorcycles especially for charity. If you look in the dictionary next to the word crazy, you will find me and my Harley motorcycle, lol. This manuscript is a book that I have worked on for 9 years. The truth is, I never wanted to publish any writing unless I could put the word doctor in front of my name as the author. Unfortunately it took me 9 painful years to earn my degree from Tennessee State University. Using *true grit* and *having authentic guts* to complete my goals; in the end I learned what it takes to become a successful educator.

APRIL'S TOP TIPS

FOR ASPIRING TEACHERS, PARENTS AND COMMUNITY PARTNERS

EXPERIMENT

If you're undecided on which path to take in life, try several paths and then decide which one is the best fit. Teaching might not be the right fit.

Ralph Waldo Emerson said, "All life is an experiment. The more experiments you make the better." Sometimes we have to step away from all things in life we have created to work on our mental health. Start over, apologize and forgive yourself first. Then move accordingly.

About the Book Cover

The collage on the front cover of *Authentic Guts,* creatively highlights a story of how even with becoming a single parent, even after divorce and living in different states, it can and it does indeed take a village to raise a child. Although not easy, with prayer, the help of grandparents, dedication, hard work and communication, co-parenting is the best chance we can give our children in reaching their full potential. We have to lead by example. How can we teach our children about overcoming obstacles, when we don't lead by example?

The outer pictures represent hours spent on the road traveling to ensure all parties were still included and involved in the well-being and success of my children. I made a decision that hurt my heart, but was necessary. I sent my son to live with his father at the between ages of 12 and 15. I knew that I could not properly raise a man and that his father's assistance was needed. And although my children have different fathers, they have always been embraced whole-heartedly in both families.

The middle photo is of me along with thousands who gathered in Washington at the Lincoln Memorial on the 57th anniversary of the Rev. Dr. Martin Luther King's "I Have a Dream" speech calling for racial justice and encouraging voting and census participation. I rode my motorcycle to join other women from across the country, California to D.C in support of our current day struggles and making a call to action for lawmakers.

The middle lower picture is a picture of my Camp Imani summer campers enjoying themselves at the top of Lookout Mountain in Chattanooga, Tennessee after a real-world social studies learning experience at Ruby Falls.

Behind the book are several pairs of hanging boxing gloves. This represents the skill, grit and courage it takes to come out of the boxing corner swinging. In our world sometimes the odds are unfavorably stacked against us. Fight like a champ and when you win, reach back, teach and inspire the youth. Prepare them and train them to think and make reasonable and sound decisions in order to become the champions they are born to be.

AUTHENTIC GUTS

REFERENCES

Adams, E., Ikemoto, G., & Taliaferro, L. (2012). Playmakers: How great principals build and lead great teams of teachers. New Leaders.

Agbo, S. A. (2007). Addressing school-community relations in a cross-cultural context: A collaborative action to bridge the gap between first nations and the school. Journal of Research in Rural Education, 22(8), 1-14 https://eric.ed.gov/?id=EJ768961

Ahmad, A. R., Adi, N., Noor, H., Rahman, A., & Yushuang, T. (2013). The influence of leadership style on job satisfaction among nurses. Asian Social Science, 9(9), 172-178. https://doi.org/10.5539/ass.v9n9p172

Ajai, J., & Imoko, I. (2013). Urban and rural students academic achievement and interest in geometry: A case study with games and simulation method. https://www.researchgate.net/publication/326093087_URBAN_AND_RURAL_STUDENTS%27_ACADEMIC_ACHIEVEMENT_AND_INTEREST_IN_GEOMETRY_A_CASE-STUDY_WITH_GAMES_AND_SIMULATIONS_METHOD

Alameda-Lawson, T., Lawson, M., & Lawson, H. (2010). Social workers' roles in facilitating the collective involvement of low-income, culturally diverse parents in an elementary school. Children & Schools, 32(3), 172-182 https://doi.org/10.1093/cs/32.3.172

Alvoid, L., & Blac, W. L. (2014). The changing role of the principal: How high achieving districts are recalibrating school leadership. https://eric.ed.gov/?id=ED561099 Anderson-Butcher, D., & Ashton, D. (2004). Innovative models of collaboration to serve children, youths, families, and communities. Children &Schools, 26(3),39-53. https://doi.org/10.1093/cs/26.1.39

Anderson, K. J., & Minke, K. M. (2007). Parent involvement in education: Toward an understanding of parents' decision making. Journal of Educational Research, 100(5), 311-323. https://www.jstor.org/stable/27548195

Andrews J.O., Newman, S.D., Meadows, O., Cox, M.J., & Bunting, S. (2012). Partnership readiness for community-based participatory research https://doi.org/10.1093/her/cyq050

Arnold, M. L., Newman, J. H., Gaddy, B. B., & Dean, C. C. (2005). A look at the con-dition of rural education research: Setting a difference for future research. Journal of Research in Rural Education, 20(6), 1-25. http://www.umaine.edu/jrre/20-6.pdf

Ary, D., Jacobs, L., Razavieh, A., & Sorensen, C. (2006). Introduction to research in education (7th ed). Thomson Wadsworth.

Ashton, B., & Duncan, H. E. (2012). A beginning rural principal's toolkit: A guide for success. Rural Educator, 34(1). https://files.eric.ed.gov/fulltext/EJ1000100.pdf

Auerbach, S. (2010). Beyond coffee with the principal: Toward leadership for authentic school-family partnerships. Journal of School Leadership, 20, 728-757.https://doi.org/10.1177/105268461002000603

Barley, Z. A., & Beesley, A. D. (2007). Rural school success: What can we learn? Journal of Research in Rural Education, 22(1). http://jrre.psu.edu/articles/22- 1.pdf

Bartling, E. M. (2013). Female high school principals in rural midwestern school districts: their lived experiences in leadership [Doctoral dissertation, University of Wisconsin-Milwaukee]. University of Wisconsin-Milwaukee Digital Commons. http://citeseerx.ist.psu.edu/viewdoc/download?doi=10.1.1.1010.8836&rep=rep1&type=pdf

Bass, B. M. (1985). Leadership and performance beyond expectations. Free Press.

Bass, B. M. (1990). From transactional to transformational leadership: Learning to share the vision. Organizational Dynamics, 18(3), 19-31. https://doi.org/10.1016/0090-2616(90)90061-S

Bass, B. M. (1998). Transformational leadership: Industrial, military, and educational impact. Erlbaum Eselman.

Bass, B. M., & Bass, R. (2008). The Bass handbook of leadership: Theory, research, and managerial applications (4th ed.). Free Press.

Belfield, C. R., &Levin, H. M. (2007). The price we pay: The costs to the nation of inadequate education. Brookings Institution Press.

Bentley, K. (2012). Principal leadership styles in an era of accountability: Self-perceived school principal leadership styles. Lap Lambert Academic Publishing. Bergeron, W. (2016). Stakeholders perspectives of factors that facilitate and hinder student success in high achieving, high poverty, high minority rural high schools in Alabama. https://end.auburn.edu/handle/10415/5395

Berry, B., Wade, C., & Trantham, P. (2009). Using data, changing teaching. Educational Leadership, 66(4), 80-84. http://www.ascd.org/publications/educational-leadeship/dec08/vol66/num04/Using-Data,-Changing-Teaching.aspx

Bifuh-Ambe, E. (2013). Developing successful writing teachers: Outcomes of professional development exploring teachers' perceptions of themselves as writers and writing teachers and their students' attitudes and abilities to write across the curriculum. English Teaching: Practice and Critique, 12(3), 137-156. https://files.eric.ed.gov/fulltext/EJ1017206.pdf

Bitsch, V. (2005). Qualitative research: A grounded theory example and evaluation criteria. Journal of Agribusiness, 23(1), 75-91. file:///C:/Users/sarah/AppData/Local/Temp/S05-05.pdf Black, G. L. (2010). Correlational analysis of servant leadership and school climate. Journal of Catholic Education, 13(4). http://dx.doi.org/10.15365/joce.1304032013

Blanchard, K. H., & Hersey, P. (1996). Great ideas revisited. Training and Development, 509(1), 42-47.

Blank, M. J., & Hanson Langford, B. (2000). Strengthening partnerships: Community school assessment checklist. Coalition for Community Schools. http://phennd.org/wp2014/wp-content/uploads/2020/04/assessment_cs.pdf

Bloomburg, L., & Volpe, M. (2008). Completing your qualitative dissertation: A roadmap from beginning to end. Sage Publications.

Bottoms, G., & O'Neil, K. (2001). Preparing a new breed of school principals: It's time for action. Southern Regional Educational Board.

Bottoms, G., & Schmidt-Davis, J. (2010). The three essentials: Improving schools requires district vision, district and state support, and principal leadership. SREB, 4. https://www.wallacefoundation.org/knowledge-center/Documents/Three-Essentials-to-Improving-Schools.pdf

Bosma, H., Johnston, M., Cadell, S., Wainwright, W., Abernethy, N., Feron, A., & Kelley, M. & Nelson, F. (2009). Creating social work competencies for practice in hospice palliative care. Palliative Medicine, 24(1), 79-87. https://doi.org/10.1177/0269216309346596

Bossert, S., Dwyer, D., Rowan, B., & Lee, G. (1982). The instructional management role of the principal. Educational Administration Quarterly, 18(3), 34-64. https://doi.org/10.1177/0013161X82018003004

Bowen, G. (2009). Supporting a grounded theory with an audit trail: An illustration. International Journal of Social Research Methodology, 12(4), 305-316. https://doi.org/10.1080/13645570802156196

Brown-Ferrigno, T. & Allen, L. W. (2006). Preparing principals for high-need rural schools: A central office perspective about collaborative efforts to transform school leadership. Journal of Research in Rural Education, 21(1), 1–16.https://jrre.psu.edu/sites/default/files/2019-08/21-1.pdf Bryan, J., & Henry, L. (2008). Strengths-based partnerships: A school–family–community partnership approach to empowering students. Professional School Counseling, 12, 149–156. https://doi.org/10.5330/PSC.n.2010-12.149

Bryman, A., & Burgess, R. (1999). Qualitative research. Sage Publications.

Budge, K. (2006). Rural leaders, rural places: Problem, privilege, and possibility. Journal of Research in Rural Education, 21(13), 1-10 https://citeseerx.ist.psu.edu/viewdoc/download?doi=10.1.1.614.1996&rep=rep1&type=pdf

Bullard, Kevin. (2008). Baba bullard speaks. Retrieved from: http://theaceschools.homestead.com/about.html

Burns, J. M. (1978). Leadership. Harper and Row.

Burton, L. M., Lichter, D. T., Baker, R. S., & Eason, J. M. (2013). Inequality, family processes, and health in the "new" rural America. American Behavioral Scientists,57(8), 1128-1151. https://doi.org/10.1177/0002764213487348

Burton, P. R., Palmer, L. J., Keen, K. J., Olson, J. M., & Elston, R. C. (2002). Response to Epstein et al. American Journal of Human Genetics, 71(2), 441–442. https://doi.org/10.1086/341663

Butler, K. (2010). Double duty: Schools as community centers. District Administration, 46(4), 50. https://districtadministration.com/toc/default.aspx

REFERENCES

California Department of Education. (2010). California preschool learning foundations: Preschool Learning Foundations, Vol. 2. https://www.cde.ca.gov/sp/cd/re/documents/psfoundationsvol2.pdf

California Department of Education. (2012). California Preschool Learning Foundations: Vol. 3 https://www.fremontchristian.com/editoruploads/files/Preschool_Learning_Foundations_Vol__3.pdf

Cambridge University Press. (2108). Cambridge academic content dictionary. https://www.campbridge.org.

Camburn, E., Rowan, B., & Taylor, J. E. (2003). Distributed leadership in schools: The case of elementary schools adopting comprehensive school reform models. Educational Evaluation and Policy Analysis, 25, 347–373 https://doi.org/10.3102/01623737025004347

Canales, M. T., Tejeda-Delgado, C., Slate, J. R. (2008). Leadership behaviors of superintendent/principals in small, rural school districts in Texas. Rural Educator, 29(3), 1-7. https://files.eric.ed.gov/fulltext/EJ869292.pdf

Canole, M., & Young, M. (2013). Standards for educational leaders: An analysis. file:///C:/Users/sarah/AppData/Local/Temp/AnalysisofLeadershipStandards.pdf

Carr, P., & Kefalas, M. (2011). Hollowing out in the middle. Beacon Press.

Carter, C. J. (2013, May 19). Why aren't low income students succeeding in school? HuffPost. https://www.huffpost.com/entry/why-arent-low-income-stud_b_2909180

Carson, J. B., Tesluk, P. E., & Marrone, J. A. (2007). Shared leadership in teams: An investigation of antecedent conditions and performance. Academy of Management Journal, 50, 1217-1234. https://doi.org/10.2307/20159921

Cavanaugh, S. (2012). Parental engagement proves no easy goal. Education Week, 31(27), 16-17. https://www.edweek.org/leadership/parental-engagement-proves-no-easy-goal/2012/04

Center for Economic and Community Development. (2019). Penn State College of Agricultural Sciences. https://www.Aese.psu.edu

Chance, E., & Lingren, C. (1989). The great plains rural secondary principal: Aspirations and reality. Research in Rural Education, 6(1), 7-11. https://jrre.psu.edu/sites/default/files/2019-07/6-1_8.pdf

Chemers, M. M. (2000). Leadership research and theory: A functional integration. Group Dynamics: Theory, Research, and Practice, 4(1), 27-43.https://doi.org/10.1037/1089-2699.4.1.27

Cherry, K. (2019). Transformational leadership: a closer look at the effects of transformational leadership. https://www.verywellmind.com/what-is-transformational-leadership-2795313

Christenson, S. L., & Reschly, A. L. (2010). Check & connect: Enhancing school completion through student engagement. In B. Doll, W. Pfohl, & J. Yoon (Eds.). Handbook of youth prevention science (pp. 327-348). Routledge.

Christie, F. (2005). Language education in the primary years. The Free Library. https://www.thefreelibrary.com/Christie%2c+F.+(2005)+Language+Education+in+the+Primary+Years.-a0153691584

Clark, D. R. (2010). Leadership styles. http://www.nwlink.com/wdonclark/leader/leadstl.html

Clawson, J. (2008). The changing context of leadership. https://www.researchgate.net/publication/228144079_The_Changing_Context_of_Leadership

Clifford, M., Hansen, U. J., & Wraight, S. (2012). A practical guide to developing comprehensive principal evaluation systems: A tool to assist in the development of principal evaluation systems. National Comprehensive Center for Quality Teaching. https://gtlcenter.org/sites/default/files/PracticalGuidePrincipalEval.pdf

Cohen, Libby G., and Spenciner, Loraine, J. (2009). Teaching students with mild and moderate disabilities. Research-based practices.

Corbett, M. (2007). Learning to leave: The irony of schooling in a coastal community. Black Point, NS: Fernwood.Cortez-Jiminez, G. (2012). Leadership needs of California rural school administrators [Unpublished doctoral dissertation]. San Diego State University. http://sdsudspace.calstate.edu/bitstream/handle/10211.10/3072/Cortez-Jiminez_Grace.pdf?sequence=1

Cosner, S. (2009). Building organizational capacity through trust. Educational Administration Quarterly, 45(2), 248-291. https://doi.org/10.1177/0013161X08330502

Council for Corporate & School Partnerships. (2009). A how-to guide for school business partnerships. https://www.doe.in.gov/sites/default/files/grants/school-business-how-guide.pdf

Council of Chief State School Officers. (2017). National conference on student assessment. www.ccsso.org

Cox-Petersen, A. (2011). Educational partnerships: Connecting schools, families, and the community. Sage Publications.

Creswell, J. W. (2003). Research design: Qualitative, quantitative, and mixed methods approaches (2nd ed.). Sage.

Creswell, J. W. (2007a). Educational research: Planning, conducting and evaluating quantitative and qualitative research (3rd ed.). Pearson.

Creswell, J. W. (2007b). Qualitative inquiry & research design: Choosing among five approaches (2nd ed.). Sage Publications.

Creswell, J. W. (2008). Educational research: Planning, conducting, and evaluating quantitative and qualitative research (3rd ed.). Pearson.

Creswell, J. W. (2009). Research design: Qualitative, quantitative, and mixed methods approaches (3rd ed.). Sage Publications.

Creswell, J. W. (2013). Qualitative inquiry & research design: Choosing among five approaches (3rd ed.). Sage Publications.

Critical Management Studies. (2016).Classical organization theory. In Organization theory (pp. 27-57). Emerald Group Publishing.

Crosnoe, R. (2009, October 1). Low-income students and the socioeconomic composition of public high schools. American Sociological Review, 74(5), 709-730. https://doi.org/10.1177/000312240907400502

Crum, K. S., & Sherman, W. H. (2008). Facilitating high achievement: High school principals' reflections on their successful leadership practices. Journal of Educational Administration, 46(5), 562-580.

REFERENCES

Crumb, L. (2020). African American Rural Education: College Transitions and Postsecondary Experiences. Emerald Publishing Limited.

Courville, K. (2018). Teacher evaluation: Challenges in rural schools. KDP Print.

Cuervo, H. (2016). Understanding social justice in rural education. Palgrave Macmillan.

Cunningham, W. G., & Cordeiro, P. A. (2006). Educational leadership: A problems-based approach (3rd ed.). Pearson.

Dawson, B. B. (2017). National rural health association policy brief. Rural community violence: An untold public health epidemic. https://www.ruralhealthweb.org/NRHA/media/Emerge_NRHA/Advocacy/Policy%20documents/2019-NRHA-Policy-Document-Rural-Community-Violence-An-Untold-Public-Health-Epidemic.pdf

Day, C., Sammons, P., Hopkins, D., Harris, A., Leithwood, K., Gu, Q., & Brown, E. (2010).10 strong claims about successful school leadership. National College for Leadership of Schools and Children's Services. https://assets.publishing.service.gov.uk/government/uploads/system/uploads/attachment_data/file/327938/10-strong-claims-about-successful-school-leadership.pdf

Day, D., & Antonakis, J. (2012). Leadership: Past, present, and future. In D. Day & J. Antonakis (Eds.), The nature of leadership (2nd ed., pp. 3-25). Sage.

Denhardt, R. B. (2004). Theories of public organization (4th ed.). Wadsworth/Thomson.

Denis, J. L., Hart, P., Hartley, J., Storey, J., & Ulrich, D. (2016). The Routledge companion to leadership. Routledge.

DiMartino, L. (2018). The role of school leaders in creating a learning ecosystem through school-community partnerships [Doctoral dissertation, Lesley University]. Educational Studies Dissertations. https://digitalcommons.lesley.edu/education_dissertations/141

Dimke, D. K. (2011). The relationship between principal leadership practices and student achievement in Illinois urban secondary schools [Unpublished doctoral dissertation]. Western Illinois University.

Dollarhide, C. T., & Lemberger, M. E. (2006). "No child left behind": Implications for school counselors. Professional School Counseling, 9(4), 295-304. https://doi.org/10.1177/2156759X0500900402

Dryfoos, J. G. (2000). Evaluations of community schools: Findings to date. Coalition for Community Schools. https://files.eric.ed.gov/fulltext/ED450204.pdf

Dufour, R., Dufour, R., Eaker, R., & Many, T. (2006). Learning by doing: A handbook for professional learning communities at work. National Education Service.

Duncan, J. G, Hirschfield, P., & Jens, L. (2000). Urban poverty and juvenile crime. Evidence from a randomized housing mobility experiment. http://www.jcpr.org/wpfiles/duncan.ludwig.revise4-25.PDF

Educating Students in Rural America. (2016). Capitalizing on strengths, overcoming barriers. National Association of State Boards of Education.

Education Alliance. (2008). Leadership in learning. http://www.EducationAlliance.org

Ehren, M. C. M., & Hatch, T. (2013). Responses of schools to accountability systems using multiple measures: The case of New York City elementary schools. Educational Assessment, Evaluation and Accountability, 25(4), 341-373. https://doi.org/10.1007/s11092-013-9175-9https://doi.org/10.1108/09578230810895492

Elliot, S., Goldring., Murphy, J., & Porter, A. (2006). Learning-centered leadership: A conceptual foundation. Vanderbilt University, TN. https://files.eric.ed.gov/fulltext/ED505798.pdf

Engaging Stakeholders. (2009). Sustaining reading first: Including parents and the community to sustain improved reading outcomes.https://www2.ed.gov/programs/readingfirst/support/stakeholderlores.pdf

Engels, N., Hotton, G., Devos, G., Bouckenooghe, D., & Aelterman, A. (2008). Principals in schools with a positive school culture. Educational Studies, 34(3), 159-174. https://doi.org/10.1080/03055690701811263

Eppley, K., Downey, J., Schulte, A. K., Azano, A. P., Brenner, D. (2020). Teaching in rural places: Thriving in classrooms, schools, and communities. Routledge.

Epstein, J. L. (1995). School/family/community partnerships: Caring for children we share. Phi Delta Kappan, 76(1). https://doi.org/10.1177/003172171009200326

Epstein, J. L. (2001). School, family and community partnerships: Preparing educators and improving schools. Westview.

Epstein, J. L. (2009). School, family, and community partnerships: Your handbook for action (3rd ed.). Corwin Press.

Epstein, J. L. (2011). School, family, and community partnerships: Preparing educators and improving schools (2nd ed.). Westview Press.

Epstein, J. L. (2019). School, family, and community partnerships: Your handbook for action (4th ed.). Sage.

Epstein, J. L., & Connors, L. J. (1992). School and family partnerships. National Association of Secondary School Principals, 1904 Research Drive, Reston VA. https://www.govinfo.gov/content/pkg/ERIC-ED467082/pdf/ERIC-ED467082.pdf

Epstein, J. L., & Sheldon, S. B. (2016). Necessary but not sufficient: The role of policy for advancing programs of school, family, and community partnerships. Journal of the Social Sciences. https://education.jhu.edu/research/article/necessary-but-not-sufficient-the-role-of-policy-for-advancing-programs-of-school-family-and-community-partnerships/

Esplin, N., Stewart, C., & Thurston, T. (2018). Technology leadership perceptions of Utah elementary school principals. Journal of Research on Technology in Education, 50(1), 1-14. https://doi.org/10.1080/15391523.2018.1487351

REFERENCES

Fairholm, M. R., & Fairholm, G. W. (2009). Understanding leadership perspectives: Theoretical and practical approaches. Springer.

Farmer, T. W., Hamm, J. V. (2016). Promoting supportive contexts for minority youth in -resource rural communities: The SEALS model, directed consultation, and the scouting report approach. In L. J. Crockett & G. Carlo (Eds.), Rural ethnic minority youth and families in the United States (pp. 247-265). Springer.

Feralzzo, L. (2011). Involvement or engagement. Educational Leadership, 68(8), 10-14. http://www.ascd.org/publications/educational-leadership/may11/vol68/num08/Involvement-or-Engagement%C2%A2.aspx

Ferguson, C. J. (2010). Genetic contributions to antisocial personality and behavior: A meta-analytic review from an evolutionary perspective. Journal of Social Psychology, 150(2),160-180. https://doi.org/10.1080/00224540903366503

Ferguson, C. J., Rueda. S., Cruz, A., Ferguson, D., Fritz, S., & Smith, S. (2008). Violent video games and aggression: Causal relationship or byproduct of family violence and intrinsic violence motivation? Criminal Justice and Behavior, 35(3), 311-332. https://doi.org/10.1177/0093854807311719

Ferguson, S. (2005). How computers make our kids stupid. Maclean's, 118(23), 24-30.

Flessa, J. (2009). Urban school principals, deficit frameworks, and implications for leadership. Journal of School Leadership, 19(3), 334-373. https://doi.org/10.1177/105268460901900304

Fletcher, A. (2005). Meaningful student involvement guide to students as partners in school change. Soundout. https://soundout.org/2015/04/02/meaningful-student-involvement-guide-to-students-as-partners-in-school-change/

Fletcher, J. K., & Kaufer, K. (2003).Shared leadership: Paradox and possibility. In C. L. Pearce & J. A. Conger (Eds.), Shared leadership: Reframing the hows and whys of leadership (pp. 27-47). Sage.

Fraenkel, J. K., & Wallen, N. E. (Eds.). (2003). How to design and evaluate research in education. McGraw-Hill.

Franklin, C., Harris, M. B., & Allen-Meares, P. (2012). The school services sourcebook: A guide for school-based professionals (2nd ed.). Oxford University Press

French, W. L. (2014). A role of the rural elementary principal: Increasing reading literacy in third graders living in poverty through advocating community partnerships (Publication No. 3643019) [Doctoral dissertation, Northwest Nazarene University]. ProQuest Dissertations and Theses Global.

Forman, M. L., Stosich, E. L., & Bocala, C. (2017). The internal coherence framework: Creating the conditions for continuous improvement in schools. Harvard Education Press.

Forner, M., Bierlein-Plamer, L., & Reeves, P. (2012). Leadership practices of effective rural superintendents: Connections to waters and Marzano's leadership correlates. Journal of Research in Rural Education, 27(8). https://eric.ed.gov/?redir=http%3a%2f%2fwww.jrre.psu.edu%2farticles%2f27-8.pdf

Foster, R., & Goddard, T. (2003). Leadership and culture in schools in northern British Columbia: Bridge building and/or re-balancing act? Canadian Journal of Educational Administration and Policy, 27. http://www.umanitoba.ca/publications/cjeap/articles/miscellaneousArticles/fostrverd.html

Georges, G. (n.d.). Downeast: Five Maine girls and the unseen story of rural America. Harper.

Given, L. M. (2008). The sage encyclopedia of qualitative research methods. Sage.

Glesne, C. (2006). Becoming qualitative researchers: An introduction. Allyn & Bacon.

Great California ShakeOut. (2010). Riverside county superintendent of schools. https://www.rcoe.us/departments/administration-and-business-services/operational-support-services/emergency-preparedness/the-great-california-shakeout

Great Schools Partnership. (2014). Glossary of education reform. https://www.greatschoolspartnership.org/resources/glossary-of-education-reform/

Greenfield, W. D. (1995). Toward a theory of school administration: The centrality of Leadership, 31(1), 61-85. https://doi.org/10.1177/0013161X95031001005

Greenleaf, R. K. (1977). Servant leadership: A journey into the nature of legitimate power and greatness. Paulist Press.

Grint, K., Holt, C., & Jones, S. (2016). What is leadership? Person, result, position, or process, or all or none of these? Routledge.

Grissom, J. A., Mitani, H., & woo, D. S. (2018). Principal preparation programs and principal outcomes. Educational Administration Quarterly, 55(1), 73-115.

Grissom, J. A., & Loeb, S. (2011). Triangulating principal effectiveness: How perspectives of parents, teachers, and assistant principals identify the central importance of managerial skills. American Educational Research Journal, 48(5), 1091-1123. https://doi.org/10.3102/0002831211402663

Gristy, C., Hargreaves, L., & Kucerova, S. R. (2020). Schools and their communities inrural Europe: Patterns of change. In L. Hargreaves, C. Gristy, & S. Kucerova (Eds.), Educational research and schooling in rural Europe: An engagement with changing patterns of education, space and place (pp. 323-338). Information Age.

Gross, J., & Hill, C. (2016). Culture in inclusive schools: Parental perspectives on family-school partnerships. Education and Training in Autism and Developmental Disabilities, 51(3), 281-293. https://www.jstor.org/stable/24827524

Groves, R. (2015, September). Rural and suburban America: When one definition is not enough. http://directorsblog.blogs.census.gov/2019/09/15/rural-and-suburban-americawhen-one-definition-is-not-enough

Guba, E. (1981). Criteria for assessing the trustworthiness of naturalistic inquiries. Educational Communication and Technology Journal, 29(2), 75- 91. https://www.jstor.org/stable/30219811

Guba, E., & Lincoln, Y. (1982). Establishing dependability and confirmability in naturalistic inquiry through an audit [Paper presentation]. Annual Meeting of the American Educational Research Association, New York, NY.

Gubrium, J. F., & Holstein, J. A. (2003). Postmodern interviewing. Sage Publications.

Gulzar, A., & Saif, M. (2012). Shared vision and partnership success. https://www.hilarispublisher.com/open-access/shared-vision-and-partnership-success-2162-6359-2-115.pdf

Gurr, D. (2017). A model of successful school leadership from the international successful school principalship project. In K. Leithwood, K., J. Sun, & K. Pollock (Eds.) How school leaders contribute to student success: The four paths framework (pp. 15-29). Springer International Publishing.

Hadfield, C. (2013). An astronaut's guide to life on Earth. Random House Canada.

Halsey, J. (2018). Independent review into regional, rural and remote education: Final report. ACT Department of Education and Training.

Hallinger, P. (2008, March). Methodologies for studying school leadership: A review of 25 years of research using the Principal Instructional Management Rating Scale [Paper presentation]. American Educational Research Association, New York, NY, United States.

Handford, V., & Leithwood, K. (2013). Why teachers trust school leaders. Journal of Educational Administration, 51(2), 194-212. https://eric.ed.gov/?redir=http%3a%2f%2fdx.doi.org%2f10.1108%2f09578231311304706

Hands, C. M. (2012). Supporting teacher leadership for partnerships. In S. Auerbach (Ed.), School leadership for authentic family and community partnerships (pp. 173-192). Routledge.

Hann, L. W. (2008). Profit and loss in school-business partnerships. District Administration, 44(5), 26-34.

Hargreaves, A., & Dennis, S. (2009). The fourth way: The inspiring future for educational change. Corwin Press.

Harmon, H. L., & Schafft, K. (2009). Rural school leadership for collaborative community development. Rural Educator, 30(3), 4-9. https://files.eric.ed.gov/fulltext/EJ869309.pdf

Harris, A., & Muijs, D. (2006). Teacher led school improvement: Teacher leadership in the UK. Teaching & Teacher Education: An International Journal of Research and Studies, 22(8), 961-972. https://doi.org/10.1016/j.tate.2006.04.010

Hartman, J. J. (2018). See the connections? Addressing leadership and supervision challenges to support improved student achievement in a small rural school. 21(3), 36-47. https://doi.org/10.1177/1555458917741172

Harvey, J., Holland, H., & Cummins, H. J. (2013). The school principal as leader: guiding schools to better teaching and learning. Perspective. https://www.wallacefoundation.org/knowledge-center/pages/the-school-principal-as-leader-guiding-schools-to-better-teaching-and-learning.aspx

Hassan, O., & Rasiah, R. (2011). Poverty and student performance in Malaysia. International Journal of Institutions and Economics, 3(1), 61-76. https://core.ac.uk/download/pdf/6293765.pdf

Heck, R. H., & Hallinger, P. (2009). Assessing the contribution of distributed leadership to school improvement and growth in math achievement. American Educational Research Journal, 46(3). https://doi.org/10.3102/0002831209340042

Henderson, A. T., Mapp, K. L. (2002). A new wave of evidence: The impact of school, family and community connections on student achievement. National Center for Family & Community Connections with Schools.

Hermann, K. R. (2016). The principal's role; distributed leadership [Doctoral dissertation, Old Dominion University]. https://digitalcommons.odu.edu/cgi/viewcontent.cgi?article=1007&context=efl_etds

Hersey, P., Blachard, K. H., & Johnson, D. E. (1996). Management of organizational behavior. Prentice-Hall International.

Hesse-Biber, S., & Leavy, P. (2006). The practice of qualitative research. Sage Publications.

Heward, William, L. (2013). Exceptional children: An introduction to special education.

Hewitt K. K., Schmidt-Davios, J., & Davis, A. W. (2018). Germinating, growing, and renewing a district-university partnership tom prepare rural school leaders. In R. M. Reardon & J. Leonard (Eds.), Innovation and implementation in rural places: School-university-community collaboration in education (pp. 29-54). Information Age.

Hill, P. T. (2014). Breaking new ground in rural education. Rural Opportunities Consortium of Idaho. http://www.rociidaho.org/wp-content/uploads/2014/11/ROCI_NewGround_Final.pdf

Hitt, D. H., & Tucker, P. D. (2016). Systematic review of key leader practices found to influence student achievement: A unified framework. Review of Educational Research, 86(2), 531-569. https://doi.org/10.3102/0034654315614911

Hnatkovska, V., & Lahiri, A. (2013). The rural-urban divide in India. http://www.theigc.org/wpcontent/uploads/2014/09/Hnatkovska-Lahiri-2012-Working-Paper-March.pdf

Hogue, M., L. (2012). A case study of perspectives on building school and community partnerships. https://scholarcommons.usf.edu/etd/4076

Holloway, I., & Wheeler, S. (2002). Qualitative research in nursing (2nd ed.). Blackwell.

Howell, W., Peterson, P., & West, M. (2013). National survey also reveals increased support for virtual schooling, support for charter schools rises sharply in minority communities. https://www.educationnext.org/ednext-poll/

Hogue, M. L. (2012). A case study of perspectives on building school and community partnerships (Doctoral dissertation). Retrieved from ProQuest Dissertations and Theses. (Accession No. 3505001)

Horng, E. L., K Daniel., & L. Susanna (2009). Principal time-use and school effectiveness. CALDER Working Paper 34. The Urban Institute.

Hunter, C., Kallio, B., & Parson, L. (2016). Exploring educational leadership in rural schools. Planning and Changing, 47(1/2), 63-81, 19.

Ingvarson, L., Anderson, M., Gronn, P., & Jackson, A. (2006). Standards for school leadership: A critical review of literature. Australian Institute for Teaching and School Leadership. https://research.acer.edu.au/cgi/viewcontent.cgi?article=1002&context=teaching_standards

Institute for Educational Leadership. (2005). Preparing leadership for rural school: Practice and policy considerations. http://www.iel/org/pubs/ruralleaders.pdf

Jacobson, S. (2011). School leadership and its effects on student achievement. International Journal of Educational Management, 25(1), 33-44.

Jago, A. G. (1982). Leadership: Perspectives in theory and research. Management Science, 28 (3), 315-336. https://doi.org/10.1287/mnsc.28.3.315

Jentz, B. C., & Murphy, J. T. (2005). Starting confused: How leaders start when they don't know where to start. Phi Delta Kappan, 86(10), 736-744. https://doi.org/10.1177/003172170508601005

Jeynes, W. H. (2005). Effects of parental involvement and family structure on the academic achievement of adolescents. Marriage & Family Review, 37(3), 99-116. http://dx.doi.org/10.1300/J002v37n03_06

Johns, J., Showalter, D., Klein, R., & Lester, C. (2014). Why rural matters 2013-2014: The condition of rural education in the 50 states. http://www.ruraledu.org/user_uploeads/file/2013-14-Why-Rural-Matters.pdf

Johnson, J., & Zoeller, B. (2016). School funding and rural districts. In S. Williams & A. Grooms (Eds.), Educational opportunity in rural contexts: The politics of place. Charlotte, NC: information Age Publishing.

Johnson, J. (2007, October). Why rural matters 2007: The realities of rural education growth. Arlington, VA: Rural School and Community Trust. http://www.ruraledu.0rg/site/apps/s/link.asp?c=beJMIZOCIrH&b=3508815

Kanungo, R., & Mendonca, M. (1996). Ethical dimensions of leadership. Sage Publications.

Karakose, T. (2008). The perceptions of primary school teachers on principal cultural leadership behaviors. Educational Sciences: Theory and Practice, 8(2), 569-579. https://files.eric.ed.gov/fulltext/EJ831168.pdf

Kelley, R. C., Thornton, B. & Daugherty, R. (2005).Relationship between measures of leadership and school climate. Education, 126(1), 17.

Khalifa, M., Arnold, N.W., & Newcomb, W. (2015). Understand and advocate for communities first. Phi Delta Kappan, 96(7), 20-25. .https://doi.org/10.1177/0031721715579035

Kingcounty.gov. (2020). Youth programs. https://www.kingcounty.gov/depts/prosecutor/youth-programs.aspx

Kouzes, J. M. (2012). The leadership challenge: How to make extraordinary things happen in organizations. Jossey-Bass.

REFERENCES

Kulatunga, A. (1990). A personal application of Kotter's definition of leadership. http://dx.doi.org/10.2139/ssrn.976167

Kythreotis, A., Pashiardis, P., & Kyriakides, L. (2010). The influence of school leadership styles and culture on students' achievement in Cyprus primary schools. Journal of Educational Administration, 48(2), 218-240.https://doi.org/0.1108/09578231011027860

Larson, C. E., & LaFasto, F. M. J. (2001). The team effectiveness questionnaire. In P.
G. Northouse (Ed.), Leadership: Theory and practice (2nd ed., p. 184). Sage.

Larson, W., & Howley, A. (2006). Leadership of mathematics reform: The role of high
school principals in rural schools. Ohio University, Appalachian Collaborative Center for Learning, Assessment, and Instruction in Mathematics. http://www.eric.ed.gov/PDFS/ED498435.pdf

Lee, M., Walker, A., & Chui, Y. L. (2012). Contrasting effects of instructional leadership practices on student learning in a high accountability context. Journal of Educational Administration, 50(5), 586-611. http://dx.doi.org/10.1108/09578231211249835

Leedy, P. D., & Ormrod, J. E. (2010) Practical research: Planning and design (9th
ed.). Merrill.

Leithwood, K. A. (2012). The Ontario leadership framework. https://www.education-leadership-ontario.ca/application/files/8814/9452/4183/Ontario_Leadership_Framework_OLF.pdf

Leithwood, K. A., Harris, A., & Hopkins, D. (2008). Seven strong claims about successful school leadership. School Leadership and Management, 28(1), 27-42. https://doi.org/10.1080/13632430701800060

Leithwood, K. A., & Mascall, B. (2009). Collective leadership effects on student achievement. Educational Administration Quarterly, 44(4), 529-561. https://doi.org/10.1177/0013161X08321221

Leithwood, K. A., & Riehl, C. (2003). What we know about successful school leadership.
Temple University, Laboratory for Student Success.

Leithwood, K., Jantzi, D., Earl, L., Watson, N., Levin, B., & Fullan, M. (2004). Strategic
leadership for large-scale reform: The case of England's national literacy and numeracy strategy. School Leadership and Management, 24(1), 57-79. https://doi.org/10.1080/1363243042000172822

Leithwood, K., Seashore, L. K., Anderson, S., & Wahlstrom, K. (2004). How leadership influences student learning. Wallace Foundation. https://www.wallacefoundation.org/knowledge-center/documents/how-leadership-influences-student-learning.pdf

Lekamge, D. (2010). Leadership roles played by school principals: An analysis of cases. Journal of Emerging Trends in Educational Research and Policy Studies, 1(2), 43-49. https://hdl.handle.net/10520/EJC135750

Lichter, D. T., & Johnson, K. M. (2007). The changing spatial concentration of America's rural poor population. Rural Sociology, 72(3), 331-358. https://doi.org/10.1526/003601107781799129

Li, D. (2004). Trustworthiness of think-aloud protocols in the study of translation processes. International Journal of Applied Linguistics, 14(3), 301-313. https://doi.org/10.1111/j.1473-4192.2004.00067.x

Lincoln, Y. S., & Guba, E. G. (1985). Naturalistic Inquiry. Sage.

Lindahl, R. A. (2010). Difference in principals' leadership behavior in high- and low-performing schools. Journal of Leadership Studies, 3(4), 34-45. https://doi.org/10.1002/jls.20137

Locke, J., & Campbell, M., & Kavanagh, D. (2012). Can a parent do too much for their child? An Examination by Parenting Professionals of the concept of overparenting. Australian Journal of Guidance and Counseling, 22(2), 249-265. https://doi.org/10.1017/jgc.2012.29

Longworth, R. (2008). Caught in the middle: America's heartland in the age of globalism. Bloomsbury.

Lynch, J. M. (2012). Responsibilities of today's principal: Implications for principal
preparation programs and principal certification policies. Rural Special Education Quarterly, 31(2), 40-47. http://dx.doi.org/10.1177/875687051203100205

Macnee, L. C., & McCabe, S. (2008). Understanding nursing research: Using research evidence-based practice. Lippincott Williams & Wilkins.

Maier, A., Daniel, J., Oakes, J., & Lam, L. (2017). Community schools as an effective
school improvement strategy: A review of the evidence. Learning Policy Institute. https://learningpolicyinstitute.org/product/community-schools-effective-school-improvement-report

Mapp, K. L., & Kuttner, P.J. (2013). Partners in education: A dual capacity-building framework for family-school partnerships. SEDL. http:/www.sedl.org/pubs/framework/

Marks, H. M. & Printy, S. M. (2003). Principal leadership and school performance: An
integration of transformational and instructional leadership. Educational Administration Quarterly, 39(3), 370-397. https://doi.org/10.1177/0013161X03258412

Marshall, C., & Rossman, G. B. (2006). Designing qualitative research (4th ed.). Sage.

Marzano, R. J., Frontier, T., & Livingston, D. (2011). Effective supervision: Supporting the art and science of teaching. Association for Supervision and Curriculum Development.

Marzano, R. J., Waters, T. & McNulty, B. A. (2005). School leadership that works: From research to results. Association for Supervision and Curriculum Development.

Maslow, A. H. (1959). Cognition of being in the peak experiences. Journal of Genetic Psychology: Research and Theory on Human Development, 94(1) 43-66.

Masumoto, M., & Brown-Welty, S. (2009). Case study of leadership practices and school-community interrelationships in high-performing, high poverty, rural California high schools. Journal of Research in rural Education, 24(1), 1-18.

Matthew, J. W. T., Schultz, T., Hannaford, N., & Runciman, W. B. (2012). Failures in transition: Learning from incidents relating to clinical handover in acute learning care. Journal of Healthcare Quality, 35(3), 49-56. https://doi.org/10.1111/j.1945-1474.2011.00189.x

Matthews, J., & Stewart, C. (2015). The lone ranger in rural education: the small rural school principal and professional development. Rural Educator, 36(3).

Mayrowetz, D. (2008). Making sense of distributed leadership: Exploring the multiple
usages of the concept in the field. Educational Administration Quarterly, 44(3), 424-435.

McKenna, M. K., & Millen, J. (2013). Look! Listen! Learn! Parent narratives and
grounded theory models of parent voice, presence, and engagement in K-12 education. School Community Journal, 23(1), 9-48.

McNeff, M. D. (2014). Preparing administrators for leadership in the rural context (Publication No. 3681105). [Doctoral dissertation, University of North Dakota]. ProQuest Dissertations & Theses Global.

REFERENCES

Meador, D. (2016). Ten ways principals can provide ongoing, collaborative teacher support. http://teaching.about.com/od/SchoolPrincipals/a/ProvideTeacher-Support.htm

Melaville, A., Berg, A. C., & Blank, M. J. (2006). Community-based learning: Engaging students for success and citizenship. Coalition for Community Schools. https://files.eric.ed.gov/fulltext/ED491639.pdf

Mertler, C. A. (2014). Action research: Improving schools and empowering educators (4th ed.). Sage.

Miles, M. B., & Huberman, A. M. (1994). Qualitative data analysis: An expanded sourcebook. Sage.

Miller, P. (2015). Leading remotely: Exploring the experiences of principals in rural and remote school communities in Jamaica. International Journal of Whole Schooling, 11(1), 35-53. https://files.eric.ed.gov/fulltext/EJ1061016.pdf

Miller, T. W. (2017). Challenges and changes in the role of superintendent of Nebraska's small rural schools. United States: university of Nebraska-Lincoln.

Mombourquette, C. (2013). Principal leadership: blending the historical perspective with the current focus on competencies in the Alberta context. Canadian Journal of Educational Administration and Policy, 147, 1-19.

Morrow, J., & Zachel, K. (2012). Through the lens of the rural lifeworld: A phenomenologicalinvestigation of the rural school principal [Unpublished doctoral dissertation]. Simon Fraser University.

Mulford, W., Silins, H., & Leithwood, K. (2004). Educational leadership for organizational learning and improved student outcomes. Kluwer Academic Press.

Murphy, J. T. (2011). Dancing in the rain: Tips on thriving as a leader in tough times, Phi Delta Kappan, 93(1), 36-41.

Nadel, W., & Sagawa, S. (2002). America's forgotten children: Child poverty in rural America. http://www.savethechildren.org/afc/afc_pdf_02.shtml

National Parent Teacher Association. (2009). PTA national standards for family-school partnerships: An implementation guide.

National Policy Board for Educational Administration (2015). Professional standards for educational leaders. https://www.wallacefoundation.org/knowledge-center/Documents/Professional-Standards-for-Educational-Leaders-2015.pdf

Neumerski, C. (2012). Rethinking instructional leadership, a review: What do we know about principal, teacher, and coach instructional leadership, and where should we go from here? Educational Administration Quarterly, 49(2), 310-347.

New Jersey Department of Education. (2017). About. www.state.nj.us

Noguera, P. (2008). The trouble with Black boys: Reflections on race, equity and the future of public education. Wiley and Sons.

Northouse, P. G. (2010). Leadership: Theory and practice (6th ed.). Sage Publications.

Okwakpam, I. N., & Okwakpam, I. O. (2012). Causes and levels of truancy among secondary school students: A case study of Rivers State, Nigeria. Problems of Education in 21st Century, 45, 51-62.

Olsen, D. D. (2018). Homegrown rural schoolteachers (Publication No. 10261198). [Doctoral dissertation, University of Iowa]. ProQuest Dissertations & Theses Global. https://ir.uiowa.edu/etd/

Olsen, G. W., & Fuller, M. L. (2008). Home-school relations: Working successfully with parents and families (3rd ed.). Pearson.

Onwuegbuzie, A. J., & Leech, N. L. (2007). Validity and qualitative research: An Oxymoron? Quality and Quantity, 41(2), 233-249.

Oregon Department of Education. (2008). Technical report: Oregon's Statewide Assessment Systems: Vol. 3. https://www.oregon.gov/ode/educator-resources/standards/Documents/volume3_standardsetting_0809.pdf

O'Reilly, C., & Waldman, D. A. (2018). Leadership for organizations. Sage. https://www.ebooks.com/en-us/book/209543282/leadership-for-organizations/david-waldman/

Paine, S., & McCann, R. (2009). Engaging stakeholders [Series]: Including parents and the community to sustain improved reading outcomes: Vol. 6. Sustaining Reading First. www2.ed.gov.

Panizzon, D. (2012). Science education in rural settings: Exploring the 'state of play' internationally. In B. J. Fraser, K. G. Tobin, & C. J. McRobbie. International handbook of science education (2nd ed., pp. 527-540). Springer.

Patterson, K. A. (2003). Servant leadership: A theoretical model [Doctoral Dissertation, Regent University]. https://www.regent.edu/wp-content/uploads/2020/12/patterson_servant_leadership.pdf

Patrikakou, E. N. (2016). Contexts of family–school partnerships: A synthesis. In S. Sheridan & K. E. Moorman (Eds.), Family-school partnerships in context. research on family-school partnerships (pp. 109-120). Springer.

Pearce, C. L., & Conger, J. A. (2003). Shared leadership: Reframing the hows and whys of leadership. Sage.

Pepper, K. (2010). Effective principals skillfully balance leadership styles to facilitate student success: A focus for the reauthorization of ESEA. Planning and Changing, 41(1/2), 42-56.

Phelps, P. H. (2008). The clearing house. Helping Teachers Become Leaders, 81(3), 119-122.

Planty, M., Provasnik, S., Hussar, W., & Snyder, T. (2007). The condition of education. National Center for Education Statistics. https://nces.ed.gov/programs/coe/

Polleys, M. S. (2002). One university's response to the anti-leadership vaccine: Developing servant leaders. Journal of Leadership Studies, 8(3), 117-130.

Porter, A., Murphy, J., Goldring, E., Elliot, S. N., Polikoff, M. S., & May, H. (2008, November 25). Vanderbilt assessment of leadership in education: Technical manual 1.0. The Wallace Foundation. www.wallacefoundation.org

Practicality. (n.d.). In Merriam-Webster online dictionary. https://www.merriam-webster.com/dictionary/practicality

Prater, D. L., Bermudez, A. B., & Owens, E. (1997). Examining parental involvement in rural, urban, and suburban schools. Journal of Research in Rural Education, 13(1), 72-75.

REFERENCES

Preston, J. P. (2008). School councils: A passing fad or future? Policy and Practice in
Education, 14(1/2), 65-84.

Preston, J. P. (2009). Educational reform via school councils: Saskatchewan's School
Community Councils as compared to an international precedent. Canadian and International Education, 38(1), 29-44.

Preston, J. P. (2010). A school council's influence on community involvement in a
Saskatchewan community [Unpublished doctoral dissertation]. University of Saskatchewan.

Preston, J. P. (2012). A school council, community involvement, and a Learning
Improvement Plan: A Saskatchewan case study. International Educational Journal: Comparative Perspectives, 11(2), 45-57.

Preston, J. P., Jakubiec, B., & Kooymans, R. (2013). Common challenges faced by rural
principals: A review of the literature. Rural Educator, 35(1).

Prentice Hall. (2012). Smith Hughes Act of 1917. http://inet.ed.gov/offices/OVAE/VocEd/InfoBoard/2.html#smithhughes

Provasnik, S., Kewal, R. A., Coleman, M. M., Gilbertson, L., Herring, W., & Xie, Q. (2007). Status of Education in Rural America (NCES 2007-040). National Center for Education Statistics, Institute of Education Science. shttps://dropoutprevention.org/wp-content/uploads/2015/05/13_Rural_School_Dropout_Issues_Report.pdf

Provini, C. (2012). Education world: Best practices for professional learning
 communities. Education World. www.educationworld.com

Redding, S., Murphy, M., & Sheley, P. (2011). Handbook on family and community
engagement. Information Age.

Reed, C. J., & Kensler, L. A.W. (2010). Creating a new system for principal preparation:
Reflections on efforts to transcend tradition and create new cultures. Journal of Research on Leadership Education, 5(12), 568-582.

Reeves, D. B. (2008). Leading to change: Effective grading practices. Educational
 Leadership, 65(5), 85–87.

Rice, K. J. (2010). Principal effectiveness and leadership in an era of accountability; What research says. https://eric.ed.gov/?id=ED509682

Roberts, C. (2010). The dissertation journey: A practical and comprehensive guide to
planning, writing and defending your dissertation. Corwin Press.

Robinson, V., Lloyd, C., & Rowe, K. (2008). The impact of leadership on student outcomes: An analysis of the differential effects of leadership types. Educational Administration Quarterly, 44(5), 635-674.

Robson, C. (2002). Real world research (2nd ed.). Blackwell Publishers.

Rost, J. (1993). Leadership development in the new millennium. Journal of Leadership Studies, 1(1), 92-110.

Roy, C. P. (2016). Increasing family engagement in an elementary school. [Doctoral dissertation, Walden University]. Walden University Dissertations and Doctoral Studies Collection. https://scholarworks.waldenu.edu/cgi/viewcontent.cgi?article=4170&context=dissertations

Rueter, J. D. (2009). Superintendent visibility: Effects on student achievement, staff accountability, and organizational culture. (Publication No. 3369182) [Doctoral dissertation]. ProQuest Dissertations and Theses Global.

Sagnak, M. (2016). Participative leadership and change-oriented organizational
citizenship: The meditating effect of intrinsic motivation. Eurasian Journal of Educational Research, 62, 181-194.

Salazar, P. S. (2007). The professional development needs of rural high school
principals. Rural Educator, 28(3). https://doi.org/10.35608/ruraled.v28i3.475

Salfi, N. (2011). Successful leadership practices of head teachers for school improvement: Some evidence from Pakistan. Journal of Educational Administration, 49(4), 414-432.

Salinas, K., Epstein, J., Sanders, M., Davis, D., & Douglas, I. (2009). Measure of school, family, and community partnerships. Northwest Regional Education Laboratory.

Sanders, M. G., & Sheldon, S. B. (2009). Principals matter: A guide to school, family,
and community partnerships. Corwin Press.

Sandholtz, J. H. (2011). Preservice teachers' conceptions of effective and ineffective
teaching practices. Teacher Education Quarterly, 38(3), 27-47.

Sanzo, K., Sherman, W., & Clayton, J. (2011). Leadership practices of successful middle school principals. Journal of Educational Administration, 49(1), 31-45. https://doi.org/10.1108/09578231111102045

Saunders, M., Lewis, P., & Thornhill, A. (2007). Research methods for business
students (4th ed.). Prentice Hall.

Sanzo, K. L., Sherman, W. H., & Clayton, J. (2011). Leadership practices of successful
middle school principals. Journal of Educational Administration, 49(1), 31-45.

Sanzo, K. L., Sherman, W. H., & Myran, S. (2010). Best practices of successful elementary school leaders. Journal of Educational Administration, 48(1), 48-63. https://doi.org/10.1108/09578231011015412

Sawati, M., Anwar, S., & Majoka, M. (2011). Principals' leadership styles and their
impact on schools' academic performance at secondary level in Khyber Paktoonkhwa, Pakistan. Interdisciplinary Journal of Contemporary Research in Business, 3(1), 1039-1049.

Schiess, J. (2015). Accountability: Rural parents believe in the promise of education, but are less confident on the delivery. file:///C:/Users/ajones41/Downloads/Rural%20Polls.pdf

Schwartz, S. H. (2012). An overview of the Schwartz theory of basic values. Online
Readings in Psychology and Culture, 2(1). https://doi.org/10.9707/2307-0919.1116

Scribner, J., Sawyer, K., Watson, S., & Myers, V. (2007). Teacher teams and distributed leadership: A study of group discourse and collaboration. Educational Administration Quarterly, 43(1), 67-100. https://doi.org/10.1177/0013161X06293631

REFERENCES

Sebastian, J., & Allensworth, E. (2012). The influence of principal leadership on classroom instruction and student learning: A study of mediated pathways to learning. Educational Administration Quarterly, 48(4), 626-663.

Sebring, P., Allensworth, E., Bryk, A., Easton, J., & Luppescu, S. (2006). The essential supports for school improvement. University of Chicago Consortium on School Research.

Semke, C. A., & Sheridan, S. M. (2012). Family-school connection in rural educational settings: A systematic review of the empirical literature. School Community Journal, 22(1), 21-47.

Shaked, H., & Schecter, C. (2017). Systems thinking for school leaders: Holistic leadership for excellence in education. Springer International.

Saunders, M., Lewis, P., & Thornhill, A. (2007). Research methods for business students (4th ed.). Prentice Hall.

Sanzo, K. L., Sherman, W. H., & Clayton, J. (2011). Leadership practices of successful middle school principals. Journal of Educational Administration, 49(1), 31-45.

Sanzo, K. L., Sherman, W. H., & Myran, S. (2010). Best practices of successful elementary school leaders. Journal of Educational Administration, 48(1), 48-63. https://doi.org/10.1108/09578231011015412

Sawati, M., Anwar, S., & Majoka, M. (2011). Principals' leadership styles and their impact on schools' academic performance at secondary level in Khyber Paktoonkhwa, Pakistan. Interdisciplinary Journal of Contemporary Research in Business, 3(1), 1039-1049.

Schiess, J. (2015). Accountability: Rural parents believe in the promise of education, but are less confident on the delivery. file:///C:/Users/ajones41/Downloads/Rural%20Polls.pdf

Schwartz, S. H. (2012). An overview of the Schwartz theory of basic values. Online Readings in Psychology and Culture, 2(1). https://doi.org/10.9707/2307-0919.1116

Scribner, J., Sawyer, K., Watson, S., & Myers, V. (2007). Teacher teams and distributed leadership: A study of group discourse and collaboration. Educational Administration Quarterly, 43(1), 67-100. https://doi.org/10.1177/0013161X06293631

Sebastian, J., & Allensworth, E. (2012). The influence of principal leadership on classroom instruction and student learning: A study of mediated pathways to learning. Educational Administration Quarterly, 48(4), 626-663.

Sebring, P., Allensworth, E., Bryk, A., Easton, J., & Luppescu, S. (2006). The essential supports for school improvement. University of Chicago Consortium on School Research.

Semke, C. A., & Sheridan, S. M. (2012). Family-school connection in rural educational settings: A systematic review of the empirical literature. School Community Journal, 22(1), 21-47.

Shaked, H., & Schecter, C. (2017). Systems thinking for school leaders: Holistic leadership for excellence in education. Springer International.

Sheldon, S., Epstein, J. L., & Galino, C. L. (2010). Not just numbers: Creating a partnership climate to improve math proficiency in schools. Leadership and Policy in Schools, 9(1), 27-48.

Sheppard, B., & Dibbon, D. (2011). Improving the capacity of school system leaders and teachers to design productive learning environments. Leadership and policy in schools. Leadership and Policy in Schools, 10(2), 125-144.

Singh, P., & Gumbi, D. (2009). Resource management skills of high school principals in rural communities. International Journal of Learning, 16(6), 249-263.

Siskar, J., & Theobald, P. (2008). Rural education. In T. Good (Ed.), 21st century education: A reference handbook (pp. 292-299). Sage.

Smarick, A., & McShane, M. (2018). No longer forgotten: The triumphs and struggles of rural education in America.

Spanneut, G., Tobin, J., & Ayers, S. (2013). Identifying the professional development needs of public-school principals based on the Interstate School Leader Licensure Consortium Standards. NASSP Bulletin, 97(1), 67-88. https://doi.org/10.1177/0192636512439230

REFERENCES

Spillane, J. P., & Diamond, J. B. (2007). Distributed leadership in practice. Teachers College Press. https://www.scholars.northwestern.edu/en/publications/distributed-leadership-in-practice

Starr, K., & White, S. (2008). The small rural school principalship: Key challenges and cross school responses. Journal of Research in Rural Education, 23(5), 1-12.

Stein, M. K., Remilliard, J. T., & Smith, M. S. (2007). How curriculum influences student learning. In F.K. Lester (Ed.), Second handbook of research on mathematics teaching and learning (pp. 319-369). Information Age.

Stockdale, A., & Macleod, M. (2013). Pre-retirement age migration to remote rural areas. Journal of Rural Studies, 32, 80–92. https://doi.org/10.1016/j.jrurstud.2013.04.009

Stockdale, D., Parsons, J., & Beauchamp, L. (2013). Instructional leadership in First Nations schools. Canadian Journal of Native Education, 36(1), 95-149.

Stone, A. G., & Patterson, K. (2005). The history of leadership focus. Servant leadership: A difference in leader focus. Leadership & Organization Development Journal, 25(4), 349-361.

Styron, R. A., Jr, & Styron, J. L. (2011). Critical issues facing school principals. Journal of College Teaching and Learning, 8(5), 1-10.

Supovitz, J., Sirinides, P., & May, H. (2010). How principals and peers influence teaching and learning. Educational Administration Quarterly, 46(1), 36-56.

Surface, J. L., & Theobald, P. (2015). What is rural school leadership? In D. Griffiths & J. P. Portelli (Eds.), Key questions for educational leaders (pp. 145-149). Word & Deed.

Taole, M. J. (2013). Exploring principals' role in providing instructional leadership in rural high schools in South Africa. Studies of Tribes and Tribals, 11(1), 75-82.

Tatum, B., &Eberlin, R., Kottraba, C., & Bradberry, T. (2003). Leadership, decision making, and organizational justice. Management Decision, 41(10), 1006-1016. https://doi.org/10.1108/00251740310509535

Teddlie, C., & Yu, F. (2007). Mixed methods sampling. Journal of Mixed Methods Research, 1(1), 77-100.

Thomas, R. (2003). Blending qualitative & quantitative research methods in theses and dissertations. Corwin Press.

Tirmizi, A. (2002). The 6-L framework: A model for leadership research and development. Leadership & Organization Development Journal, 23(5), 269-279.

Tobin, G. A., & Begley, C. M. (2004). Methodological rigor within a qualitative framework. Journal of Advanced Nursing, 48(4), 388-396.

Tobin, P. D. (2017). A rural superintendent's challenges and rewards. www.aasa.org

Tomervik, K. (1995). Workforce diversity in Fortune 500 corporations headquartered in Minnesota: Concepts and practices. Academy of Human Resource Development (AHRD) Conference Proceedings, St. Louis, MO.

Tran, H. (2017). The impact of pay satisfaction and school achievement on high school principals' turnover intentions. Educational Management.

Tuoti, G., & Sanna, J. (2016), April 11). Many factors contribute to principal turnover. The Arlington Advocate. Retrieved from http://arlington.wickedlocal.com/article/20120160/news/16041978

U.S. Department of Education. (2011). Small rural achievement program. http://www2.ed.gov/programs/reapsrsa/eligibility.html

U.S. Department of Education, Fundamental Change. (2015). Innovation in America's schools under race to the top. https://www2.ed.gov/programs/racetothetop/rttfinalrpt1115.pdf

U.S. Department of Education, Office for Civil Rights. (2015). Title IX and sex discrimination. https://www2.ed.gov/about/offices/list/ocr/docs/tix_dis.htm l

Census Bureau. (2015). American community survey, 5 year estimates 2011-2015. https://www.census.gov/library/visualizations/2016/comm/acs-ruralurban.html.

van Eekelen, W. (2020). Rural development in practice: Evolving challenges and opportunities. Taylor & Francis.

Viadero, D. (2008). Exercise seen as priming pump for students' academic strides. Education Week, 27(23), 14-25.

Vincent, J. M. (2018). Small districts, big challenges: Barriers to planning and funding school facilities in California's rural and small public school districts. center for cities + schools. https://files.eric.ed.gov/fulltext/ED586248.pdf

Vito, G., & Higgins, G., & Denney, A. (2014). Transactional and transformational leadership. Policing: An International Journal of Police Strategies & Management, 37(4), 809-822. https://doi.org/10.1108/PIJPSM-01-2014-0008

Walsh, M., & Backe, S. (2013). School–university partnerships: Reflections and opportunities. Peabody Journal of Education,88(5), 594-607. https://doi.org/10.1080/0161956X.2013.835158

Warner, M. J., & Williams, E. F. (2006). Inspiring leadership: It's not about the power. Pearson Custom Publishing.

Waters, J., Marzano, R., & McNulty, B. (.2003). Balanced leadership: What 30 years of research tell us about the effect of leadership on student achievement. Mid-Continent Research for Education and Learning. https://files.eric.ed.gov/fulltext/ED481972.pdf

Wengraf, T. (2001). Qualitative research interviewing. Sage Publications.

White, D. (2015). A qualitative study of professional learning communities and rural student achievement. North Central University.

Whittemore, R., Chase, S., & Mandle, C. (2001). Validity in qualitative research: Pearls, pith and provocation. Qualitative Health Research, 11(4), 522–537.

REFERENCES

Williams, K. C., & Williams, C. C. (2011). Five key ingredients for improving student motivation. Research in Higher Education Journal, 12(1), 11-12.
Wise, B. (2010). America's rural high schools: Challenges and opportunities for success. https://all4ed/wpcontent/uploads/2010/02/RuralHSReportChallengesOpps.pdf
Witten, M. (2010). Building the community school: How school principals can lead in addressing educational and social challenges in South Africa (Publication No. 3446318). [Doctoral dissertation, Harvard University]. Proquest Dissertations and Theses Global.
Wood, L., Bauman, E., Rudo, Z., & Dimock, V. (2017). How family, school, and community engagement can improve student achievement and influence school reform.
Wormser, Richard. (2002). The rise and fall of jim crow. Retrieved from: http://www.pbs.org/wnet/jimcrow/stories_people_dubois.html

https://www.nmefoundation.org/getattachment/67f7c030-df45-4076-a23f-0d7f0596983f/Final-Report-Family-Engagement-AIR.pdf?lang=en-US&ext=.pdf
Xenikou A. (2017). Transformational leadership, transactional contingent reward, and organizational identification: The mediating effect of perceived innovation and goal culture orientations. Frontiers in Psychology, 18(8), Article 1754. https://doi.org/10.3389/fpsyg.2017.01754
Yang, Y. (2014). Principals' transformational leadership in school improvement. International Journal of Educational Management, 28, 77-83. https://doi.org/10.1108/IJEM-04-2013-0063
Yener, S. (2020). Participative leadership: A handbook of leadership styles. https://www.academia.edu/44655560/A_Handbook_of_Leadership_Styles
Yentes, J., & Gaskill, M. (2015). Technology use in rural and urban schools: Challenges and opportunities in the Midwest. In D. Slykhuis & G. Marks (Eds.), Proceedings of Society for Information Technology & Teacher Education International Conference (pp. 1415-1423). Association for the Advancement of Computing in Education. http://www.editlib.org/p/150581
Yin, R. K. (2009). Case study research: Design and methods (4th ed.). Sage Publishing.
Yin, R. K. (2014). Case study research: Design and methods (5th ed.). Sage Publications.
Yukl, G. (2010). Leadership in organizations. Pearson.
Zhang, T., Avery, G. C., Bergsteiner, H., & More, E. (2014). The relationship between leadership paradigms and employee engagement. Journal of Global Responsibility, 5(1), 4-21.
(2013). NNDB tracking the world. Retrieved from: http://www.nndb.com/people/535/000031442/

Ajamu, A., Parham, T., & White, J. L. (1999). The psychology of blacks; an african centered prospective.
Ani, M. (1994). Yurugu: An African centered critique of European cultural thought and behavior. Trenton N.J: Africa Word Press.
Asante, M. (1987). The afrocentric idea. Philadelphia: Temple Press.
Betty Shabazz International Charter School. (1998). Welcome page. Retrieved 2 22, 2011, from Betty Shabazz: www.bsics.net
Bullard, B. (2009). Baba Bullard speaks on educational malpractice: The Maafa revisited. Habari Gani, 1.
Carruthers, J. H. (1999). Intellectual warfare.
Journal of Black Studies 2020, Vol. 51(1) 3–15. The Author(s) 2019 Article reuse guidelines: sagepub.com/journals-permissions DOI: 10.1177/0021934719892236journals.sagepub.com/home/jbs
Department of Political Science, Clark Atlanta University, Atlanta, GA, United States, timothy.williams@students.cau.edu
Montero, Maritza (2014)."Encyclopedia of Critical Psychology", Springer New York, New York, NY",
pages="296--299",

Clark, J. H. (1994). Education for a new reality in the african world.
Goggins, E. &. (1986). High school science enrollment of black studnets. Journal of Research in Science Teaching., 23, 251-62.
Goggins, L. (1996). African centered rites of passage and education. Chicago: African American Images.
Goggins, L. (2003). The Academic Stars Retention Model: An Empirical investigation of its Effectiveness. The University of Akron, Graduate Department. Akron: University of Akron Office of Research.
Hale-Benson, J. E. (1986). Black children: their roots, cultures and learning styles.
hilliard, A. D. (1997). SBA: the re-awakening of the african mind.
hilliard, A. D. (1998). African power: affirming african indigenous socialization in the face of culture wars.
Irvine, J. (1991). Black students and school failure. New York: Praeger Publishers.
James, G. G. (2009). Stolen legacy.
Kunjufu, J. (2000). Developing positive self-image and discipline in black children.
Kunjufu, J. (2008). 100+ educational strategies to teach children.
Kush, K. I. (2000). What they never told you in hiustory class.
Ladson-Billings, G. (1994). the dreamkeepers: Successful teachers of africanamerican children.
Lewis, A. E. (2003). Race in the schoolyard: Negotiating the color line in classrooms and communitites.
Nobles, W. W. (1986). African psychology: Towards its reclamation, reascension and revitalization.
Perry, t., & Steele, c. a. (2003). Young, gifted and black: promoting high achievement among africanamerican students.
Sertima, I. V. (2003). They came before columbus: the african presence in ancient america.
Shuttleworth, M. (2008). Experiment Resources. Retrieved 4 19, 2011, from Null Hypothesis: http://www.experiment-resources.com/null-hypothesis.html
Stanton-Salazar, R. &. (2000). The network orientation of highly resilient urban minority youth: A network - analytic account of minority socialization and its educational implications. The Urban Review, 227-261.
Tedla, E. (1996). Sankofa: African thought and education. New York: Peter Lang.
Thompson, G. L. (2004). Through ebony eyes; what teachers need to know but are afraid to ask about african-american students.
Welsing, F.-C. D. (1991). The isis papers; the keys to the colors.
Wilson, A. N. (1992). Awakening the natural genius of black children.
Wortham, A. (1992). Afrocentrism isn't the answer for black students in American society. The Education Digest, 58, 63-66.
Yin, R. K. (1984). Case study research; design and methods. Newbury Park, CA: Sage.